GLOBAL BRANDS

**ED. JULIUS
WIEDEMANN**

LOGO DESIGN

— GLOBAL BRANDS —

TASCHEN

Bibliotheca Universalis

CONTENTS

FROM LOGO DESIGN TO GLOBAL BRANDS
A SURVEY OF TODAY'S VISUAL CULTURE

INTRODUCTION
JULIUS WIEDEMANN

More than 50 percent of the world's GDP is accounted for today by the turnover of larger corporations. What technology and international logistics have made possible is unprecedented in terms of how all manner of products can be made available to billions of people worldwide and almost instantaneously. Brands now operate across dozens of different cultures, millions of points of sales, and are advertised in countless media outlets. The importance of corporate identity has always been undeniable, but in a globalized environment perceptions such as trust, quality, reliability, productivity, and so on are more often than not conveyed through symbols rather than words.

The reason why global brands are important, both visually and also economically, is that companies are aware of the need to ensure that their employees all feel that they belong to one place. In this sense, corporate identity helps make clear that the workers are part of a team. Truly global brands first started to flourish at the beginning of the 20th century at a time when businesses became able to export their wares to multiple destinations, on a massive scale, thanks to huge improvements in transportation and communication, which then led to a need for brands to demonstrate the coherence between their various products. Mass production also meant the creation of standards for the items being made in large numbers, which in turn helped make the whole process of sales and marketing more efficient. Global visual identities became indispensable and it has frequently been the case that certain design firms work solely in this area.

In contrast to today, when local and hand-made products are increasingly valued, most of the last century was characterized by the widespread industrialization of production of food, medicine, household items, cars, etc., and also the initiative of businesses to cross international boundaries in order to get these products sold, from advertising agencies through to transportation and financial services. At the same time, sport, music, and the rest of the entertainment industry also went global, which offered huge opportunities for design to represent these areas and play a major role in our understanding of culture.

When we think about global brands today we tend to picture consumer products that are widely available worldwide, such as Kellogg's cornflakes, Coca-Cola, Kit Kat, Apple computers, or Microsoft software. But there are countless businesses, large and small, that survive by exporting to multiple countries a range of brands that are completely unknown to the vast majority of people. If you're selling an aviation detergent from Germany to 30 different countries, or if your business is exporting mangoes from the Philippines, that makes you a global company and you have a global brand. As such you will want to make sure that wherever your product is shipped to and sold it complies with all the regulations of the local authorities as well as using the local language for both its packaging and instructions. But you will also probably want to ensure that your product is recognized within the industry of which it forms a part, and which will often be dispersed throughout a number of different countries.

Another important aspect of global brands is that they evolve. Bigger companies acquire smaller ones both at home and in other countries, and more often than not they then feel a need to implement a new visual identity. This often ends up being a combination of local names with visual symbols that were designed for international use. For instance, Nestlé has acquired dozens of ice-cream brands from around the world, and has unified the visual symbols that represent them while retaining the local name. In doing so, the careful use of typography has also become an integral part of keeping a range of individual identities under the main umbrella brand, with many companies achieving this by commissioning a brand-wide customized typography.

"The reason why global brands are important, both visually and also economically, is that companies are aware of the need to ensure that their employees all feel that they belong to one place. In this sense, corporate identity helps make clear that the workers are part of a team."

The branding agency market that supplies services to companies playing the global game is a multi-billion-dollar industry. For a long time it took second place behind the advertising industry, specifically because it was less closely linked to the sales of the actual products. With consumer behavior changing at such a rapid pace in the wake of advances in technology and the enormous democratization of

communication tools, brands are now more important than ever. The *New York Times* and the *Washington Post*, for example, which used to be only North American newspapers, are now global brands that are sold worldwide. The business of managing a global brand entails a number of high-level risks, thus raising the level of responsibility of the brand managers in question. What might only be a little problem with a brand close to its source could develop into a huge problem in its export destinations. So, with brand diffusion comes brand awareness, and this again is a reason why businesses sometimes undergo rebranding.

Another aspect of branding in the global context is that brands can get old. Logomarks and logotypes are not just quick identifiers, they communicate with their market and also with the time in which they appear. At regular intervals most companies feel the need to re-imagine what they represent, both for their customers, but also for their employees. Branding plays a fundamental part in this process, and although it might sound a cliché, the logo is the vehicle through which people are enabled to understand a unified message. In some cases large companies might acquire smaller ones in other countries and take years to adopt the local identity. However, it's only then that their employees feel that they actually work for the same corporation, simply because there is a symbol that unifies the understanding of who the employer is, and also that they belong to the same team.

This book aims to cover not only international consumer products that are well known to the wider public, but also brands from more niche industries which, despite their own international market and share of the world's GDP, are still unknown to most people. The purpose of a survey of this sort is to offer a tool for anyone interested in the subject so that they may gain a better glimpse into the sheer diversity of global branding. Furthermore, it should help to give a better idea of the substantial number of globalized firms that are unknown but which contribute to the field of brand design.

Julius Wiedemann studied graphic design and marketing and was an art editor for newspapers and design magazines in Tokyo before joining TASCHEN in 2001. His titles include the Illustration Now! *and* Record Covers *series, as well as the infographics collection and books about advertising and visual culture.*

VOM LOGO DESIGN ZU GLOBAL BRANDS
EIN ÜBERBLICK ÜBER DIE HEUTIGE VISUELLE KULTUR

EINLEITUNG
JULIUS WIEDEMANN

Mehr als 50 Prozent des weltweiten BIP entfallen heute auf den Umsatz größerer Unternehmen. Was Technologie und internationale Logistik möglich gemacht haben, ist beispiellos in Bezug darauf, wie verschiedenste Produkte Milliarden von Menschen weltweit und nahezu sofort zugänglich gemacht werden können. Marken wirken mittlerweile in Dutzenden verschiedenen Kulturen und werden an Millionen von Verkaufspunkten vertreten und von unzähligen Medienunternehmen beworben. Die Bedeutung der Corporate Identity war immer unstrittig aber in einem globalisierten Umfeld werden Begriffe wie Vertrauen, Qualität, Zuverlässigkeit, Produktivität usw. häufig durch Symbole anstelle von Wörtern vermittelt.

Darum ist es wichtig, dass die Unternehmen der globalen Marken sowohl visuell als auch wirtschaftlich der Notwendigkeit bewusst sind und sicherstellen, dass alle ihre Mitarbeiter das Gefühl bekommen, dass sie zu einem Ganzen gehören. In diesem Sinne hilft die Corporate Identity dabei, den Mitarbeitern zu vermitteln, dass sie Teil eines Teams sind. Wirklich globale Marken hatten ihre Blütezeit zu Anfang des 20. Jahrhunderts, zu einer Zeit, als es für Unternehmen plötzlich möglich war, ihre Waren in großem Umfang an verschiedene Ziele zu exportieren. Dies gelang dank erheblicher Verbesserungen in den Bereichen Transport und Kommunikation und führte dazu, dass Marken die Kohärenz ihrer verschiedenen Produkte nachweisen mussten. Massenproduktion bedeutete auch die Schaffung von Standards für die Artikel, die in großen Stückzahlen gefertigt

wurden, was wiederum dazu beitrug, den gesamten Verkaufs- und Marketingprozess effizienter zu gestalten. Globale und visuelle Identitäten wurden zu einem unverzichtbaren Element und häufig arbeiteten bestimmte Designbüros ausschließlich in diesem Bereich.

Im Gegensatz zu heute, da lokale und handgefertigte Produkte wieder mehr geschätzt werden, war der Großteil des letzten Jahrhunderts durch die weit verbreitete Industrialisierung der Produktion von Nahrungsmitteln, Medikamenten, Haushaltsgegenständen, Autos usw. gekennzeichnet und auch durch die Initiative von Unternehmen, internationale Grenzen zu überschreiten, um diese Produkte zu verkaufen. Dies betraf Werbeagenturen bis hin zu Transport- und Finanzdienstleistungsunternehmen. Gleichzeitig wurden auch Sport, Musik und der Rest der Unterhaltungsindustrie global ausgerichtet, was dem Design enorme Möglichkeiten bot, diese Bereiche zu repräsentieren und eine wichtige Rolle in unserem Kulturverständnis zu spielen.

Wenn wir heute an globale Marken denken, neigen wir dazu, uns Konsumgüter vorzustellen, die auf der ganzen Welt erhältlich sind, z.B. Kelloggs Cornflakes, Coca-Cola, Kit Kat, Apple-Computer oder Microsoft-Software. Es gibt jedoch unzählige große und kleine Unternehmen, die dadurch überleben, dass sie eine Reihe von Marken in verschiedene Länder exportieren und die der großen Mehrheit der Menschen völlig unbekannt sind. Wenn Sie ein Flugzeugreinigungsmittel aus Deutschland in 30 verschiedene Länder verkaufen oder wenn Ihr Unternehmen Mangos von den Philippinen exportiert, macht Sie das zu einem globalen Unternehmen und Sie haben eine globale Marke. Daher sollten Sie sicherstellen, dass Ihr Produkt, überall wo es ausgeliefert und verkauft wird, den Vorschriften der örtlichen Behörden entspricht und dass sowohl die Verpackung als auch die Anweisungen in der jeweiligen Landessprache sind. Wahrscheinlich möchten Sie aber auch sicherstellen, dass Ihr Produkt in der Branche, von der es ein Teil ist, anerkannt und in verschiedenen Ländern vertrieben wird.

»Darum ist es wichtig, dass die Unternehmen der globalen Marken sowohl visuell als auch wirtschaftlich der Notwendigkeit bewusst sind und sicherstellen, dass alle ihre Mitarbeiter das Gefühl bekommen, dass sie zu einem Ganzen gehören. In diesem Sinne hilft die Corporate Identity dabei, dass die Mitarbeiter das Gefühl bekommen, Teil eines Teams zu sein.«

Ein weiterer wichtiger Aspekt globaler Marken ist, dass sie sich weiterentwickeln. Größere Unternehmen erwerben kleinere Unternehmen sowohl im In- als auch im Ausland und in den meisten Fällen besteht dann das Bedürfnis nach einer neuen visuellen Identität. Dies führt oft zu einer Kombination aus lokalen Namen mit visuellen Symbolen, die für den internationalen Gebrauch konzipiert wurden. Zum Beispiel hat Nestlé Dutzende von Eismarken auf der ganzen Welt erworben und die

visuellen Symbole vereinigt, die sie repräsentieren, wobei der lokale Name beibehalten wurde. Dabei ist der sorgfältige Gebrauch der Typografie zu einem festen Bestandteil geworden, um eine Reihe von individuellen Identitäten unter der Dachmarke zu halten. Viele Unternehmen erreichen dies, indem sie eine für die gesamte Marke passende, individuelle Typografie in Auftrag geben.

Der Markt für Branding-Agenturen, die Dienstleistungen für global agierende Unternehmen anbieten, ist eine Multi-Milliarden-Dollar-Industrie. Lange Zeit rangierte das Branding hinter der Werbebranche an zweiter Stelle, zumal es weniger eng mit dem Verkauf der eigentlichen Produkte verbunden war. Da sich das Konsumverhalten im Zuge des technologischen Fortschritts und der enormen Demokratisierung der Kommunikationsmittel so schnell verändert, sind Marken heute wichtiger denn je. Die *New York Times* und die *Washington Post* zum Beispiel, die lange Zeit nur rein nordamerikanische Zeitungen waren, sind jetzt globale Marken, die weltweit verkauft werden. Das Management einer globalen Marke ist mit einer Reihe von Risiken verbunden, wodurch die Verantwortung der betreffenden Markenmanager erhöht wird. Was nur ein kleines Problem mit einer Marke in der Nähe ihrer Quelle sein könnte, könnte sich unter Umständen in den Exportzielen zu einem riesigen Problem entwickeln. Mit der Markendiffusion geht also die Bekanntheit der Marke einher. Dies ist wiederum ein Grund, warum sich Unternehmen manchmal umbenennen.

Ein weiterer Aspekt des Brandings im globalen Kontext ist, dass Marken alt werden können. Graphiken und Schriftzüge sind nicht nur schnelle Identifikatoren, sie kommunizieren mit ihrem Markt und auch mit der Zeit, in der sie erscheinen. In regelmäßigen Abständen haben die meisten Unternehmen das Bedürfnis, sich und das was sie repräsentieren neu darzustellen, sowohl für ihre Kunden als auch für ihre Mitarbeiter. Branding spielt in diesem Prozess eine grundlegende Rolle. Auch wenn es sich nach einem Klischee anhört, ist das Logo das Mittel, durch das die Menschen eine einheitliche Botschaft verstehen können. In einigen Fällen erwerben große Unternehmen möglicherweise kleinere Unternehmen in anderen Ländern und brauchen Jahre, um die lokale Identität zu übernehmen. Nur dann haben die Mitarbeiter das Gefühl, tatsächlich für ein und dasselbe Unternehmen zu arbeiten, einfach, weil es ein Symbol gibt, welches das Verständnis darüber eint, wer der Arbeitgeber ist und sie zum selben Team gehören.

Dieses Buch soll nicht nur die internationalen Konsumgüter behandeln, die der breiten Öffentlichkeit bekannt sind, sondern wird auch Marken aus Nischenindustrien vorstellen, die trotz ihres eigenen internationalen Marktes und deren Anteil am weltweiten BIP den meisten Menschen noch unbekannt sind. Zweck einer solchen Erhebung ist es, allen Interessierten ein Instrument anzubieten, um einen besseren Einblick in die Vielfalt des globalen Brandings zu bekommen. Darüber hinaus soll es dazu beitragen, eine bessere Vorstellung von der großen Anzahl globalisierter Unternehmen zu vermitteln, die weniger bekannt sind, jedoch zum Markendesign beitragen.

Julius Wiedemann studierte Grafikdesign und Marketing und arbeitete in Tokio als Kunstredakteur für digitale Medien und Designmagazine. Seit 2001 ist er Editor bei TASCHEN, zu seinen Titeln zählen Serien wie Illustration Now!, *Sammlungen von Plattencovern und Informationsgrafiken sowie Bücher über Werbung und visuelle Kultur.*

DE LA CONCEPTION DU LOGO AUX MARQUES MONDIALES
UN SURVOL DE LA CULTURE VISUELLE D'AUJOURD'HUI

INTRODUCTION
JULIUS WIEDEMANN

À l'heure actuelle, le chiffre d'affaires des grandes sociétés cumule plus de 50 % du PIB mondial. La technologie et la logistique à l'échelle internationale ont conféré la capacité inédite de distribuer n'importe quel type de produit, de façon quasi instantanée, à des milliards de personnes à travers la planète. Les marques opèrent aujourd'hui au sein de dizaines de cultures, sur des millions de points de vente, et leur promotion se fait via d'innombrables médias. L'image de marque a toujours revêtu une importance indéniable, mais dans un environnement globalisé, la perception de confiance, de qualité, de fiabilité ou encore de productivité se traduit plutôt par le biais de symboles que de mots.

Les marques mondiales sont importantes sur le plan tant visuel qu'économique, car les entreprises savent qu'elles doivent procurer à leurs employés le sentiment d'appartenance à une structure : à cette fin, l'image de marque indique clairement que les travailleurs sont membres d'une équipe. Les marques véritablement mondiales ont commencé à prospérer au début du XXᵉ siècle, à l'époque où les compagnies ont pu exporter leurs biens à diverses destinations et à grande échelle grâce aux énormes progrès en matière de transports et de communications ; les marques ont alors ressenti le besoin de prouver la cohérence entre leurs produits. La production de masse a également motivé l'élaboration de normes pour les articles fabriqués en grandes quantités, d'où une efficacité accrue du processus de ventes et marketing dans son ensemble. Les identités visuelles globales sont devenues incontournables

et bien souvent, certains agences de design se sont consacrées exclusivement à ce domaine.

Comparé à aujourd'hui, où les produits locaux et faits main sont chaque fois plus appréciés, la majeure partie du siècle dernier s'est caractérisée par l'industrialisation généralisée de la production d'aliments, de médicaments, d'articles ménagers, de véhicules, etc., ainsi que par l'initiative des entreprises de franchir les frontières pour vendre ces produits à l'étranger, des agences de publicité aux services financiers et aux sociétés de transport. En parallèle, le monde du sport, de la musique et le reste de l'industrie du spectacle se sont également globalisés, offrant ainsi au design d'immenses opportunités de représenter ces domaines et de jouer un rôle clé dans notre compréhension de la culture.

Lorsqu'il est question de marques mondiales de nos jours, nous pensons normalement à des produits de consommation disponibles dans le monde entier, qu'il s'agisse de pétales de maïs Kellogg's, de Coca-Cola, de Kit Kat, d'ordinateurs Apple ou de logiciels Microsoft. Mais il existe un nombre infini d'entreprises, petites ou grandes, qui survivent en exportant à divers pays une série de marques totalement inconnues de la vaste majorité du public. Si depuis l'Allemagne vous vendez dans 30 pays un détergent utilisé en aviation ou si vous exportez des mangues depuis les Philippines, votre société est globale, tout comme votre marque. Dans ce cas, vous devez vous assurer que partout où votre produit est expédié et vendu, il est conforme à toutes les réglementations des autorités locales, et que tant son emballage comme les instructions qui y figurent sont dans la langue de l'endroit. Votre produit doit aussi être reconnu au sein de son secteur, sachant qu'il sera souvent distribué dans divers pays.

« Les marques mondiales sont importantes sur le plan tant visuel qu'économique, car les entreprises savent qu'elles doivent procurer à leurs employés le sentiment d'appartenance à une structure : à cette fin, l'image de marque indique clairement que les travailleurs sont membres d'une équipe. »

Les marques mondiales connaissent par ailleurs une évolution. Les grandes sociétés en acquièrent de plus petites tant sur le marché national qu'à l'étranger et, la plupart du temps, elles souhaitent afficher une nouvelle identité visuelle : celle-ci s'obtient souvent en combinant des noms locaux et des symboles visuels conçus pour un usage international. Nestlé a par exemple racheté des dizaines de marques de glace du monde entier et unifié les choix visuels les symbolisant tout en conservant leur appellation locale. L'emploi soigné de la typographie est devenu en cela un garant de la conservation d'une série d'identités individuelles sous la marque ombrelle, nombre de sociétés s'y prêtant en recourant à une typographie personnalisée appliquée à l'ensemble de leur marque.

Le marché des agences de branding, qui fournit des services aux sociétés présentes sur la scène mondiale, brasse des milliards de dollars. Il a pendant longtemps occupé la deuxième place derrière la sphère publicitaire, principalement car il était moins étroitement lié à la vente de produits. Avec l'évolution rapide du comportement des consommateurs, les progrès technologiques et l'immense démocratisation des outils de communication, les marques sont désormais plus importantes que jamais. Le *New York Times* et le *Washington Post* par exemple sont passés d'être des journaux nord-américains à des marques mondiales vendues dans le monde entier. La gestion d'une marque mondiale suppose des risques élevés, ce qui augmente le niveau de responsabilité des chefs de marque concernés.

Un problème peut rester mineur avec une marque proche de son origine mais prendre une grande envergure sur les lieux de destination. Par conséquent, la diffusion des marques a supposé leur notoriété, autre raison pour laquelle les entreprises sont parfois amenées à renouveler leur branding.

Dans le contexte global, le branding se voit également motivé par le vieillissement des marques. Les blocs-marques et les logotypes sont bien plus que de simples identifiants : ils communiquent avec leur marché et leur époque. Régulièrement, les entreprises ressentent le besoin de repenser ce qu'elles représentent, tant pour leurs clients que pour leurs employés. Le branding joue un rôle fondamental dans ce processus et même si ceci peut sembler un cliché, le logo est le vecteur par lequel les gens peuvent comprendre un message unifié. Parfois, de grandes entreprises en achètent de plus petites dans d'autres pays et mettent des années à adopter l'identité locale ; c'est toutefois seulement à ce

moment-là que leurs employés ont la
sensation de travailler pour la même organisation, tout bonnement parce qu'un symbole unifie la vision de qui est l'employeur
et qu'ils appartiennent à la même équipe.
    Cet ouvrage vise à aborder non seulement
les produits de consommation internatio-
naux connus du grand public, mais aussi les
marques de niches qui, malgré leur présence
à l'international et leur part du PIB mondial,
restent inconnues de la majorité de la popu-
lation. L'objectif d'un recueil de ce type est
de permettre aux personnes intéressées par le
sujet de se faire une meilleure idée de la
grande diversité du branding global. Il doit
en outre aider à découvrir le nombre
conséquent de sociétés globalisées qui, bien
qu'inconnues, jouent un rôle dans le
domaine du design de marques.

*Julius Wiedemann a étudié le graphisme
et le marketing. Avant de rejoindre TASCHEN
en 2001, il fut le directeur artistique de
journaux et magazines spécialisés dans le design
à Tokyo. Parmi ses titres figurent les séries*
Illustration Now! *et* Record Covers, *la
collection de livres sur l'infographie et des
ouvrages sur la publicité et la culture visuelle.*

CONSUMER PRODUCTS & RETAIL

BICYCLES
CHILDREN CARE
CONSUMER RETAIL
HEALTH & BEAUTY
HOME APPLIANCES
HOME CARE
IMAGING & PHOTOGRAPHIC
KITCHENWARE
OFFICE SUPPLIES
PERSONAL CARE
TOBACCO
TOYS

Columbus Tubi
Italy

Fuji Bikes
USA

Schwalbe
Germany

GT Bicycles
USA

Trek
USA

Scott Sports
Switzerland

Roadmaster Bike
USA

cannondale

Cannondale
USA

SCHWINN

Schwinn
USA

YAMAGUCHI

Yamaguchi Bicycles
USA

SHIMANO

Shimano
USA

GIANT

Giant
Taiwan

Cinelli
Italy, 1979
Italo Lupi

Specialized
USA

Super Mario Bros
(Mushroom Kingdom)
Japan

Giochi Preziosi
Italy

K'Nex
USA

Wham-O
USA

Kyosho
Japan

Colorforms
USA, 1959
Paul Rand

Little Tikes
USA

Duplo
Denmark, 2004

Lego
Denmark, 1998

Klein
Germany

Gunica
South Korea

Toys "R" Us
USA, 2007

Hasbro
USA, 2009

Barbie
USA, 2004

Schuco
Germany

Playmobil
Germany

Bburago
Italy, 1976

Tamiya
Japan

Tonka
USA

Hornby
United Kingdom, ca 1996

Playskool
USA

Play-Doh
USA

ToyBiz
Canada, ca 1988

Mattel
USA, 1970

Ravensburger
Germany, 1974

Mega Bloks
Canada

Revell
USA, 2007

Fisher-Price
USA, 1984

Scrabble
USA

Johnny Lightning
USA

Monopoly
United Kingdom, 2008

Quercetti
Italy

Monopoly
USA

Hasbro
USA, 1980s

Hello Kitty
Japan, 1974
Yuko Shimizu (character)

IRWIN

Irwin Toy Limited
Canada

TOMY

Tomy
Japan, ca 1979

TOMY

Tomy
Japan

TYCO

Tyco Toys
USA

Crayola

Crayola
USA, 1968

Kenner
USA

NIKKO

Nikko
Japan

Steiff
Germany

RM
Germany

Worlds of Wonder
USA, 1980s

LeapFrog
USA

Fred & Friends
USA

Action Man
United Kingdom

Hot Wheels
USA, 1968
Rick Irons

G.I. Joe
USA

Matchbox
USA

Meccano
France

Micro Machines
USA

Hirobo Limited
Japan

Aibo
Japan

Pampers
USA, 2001

Chicco
Italy

Cam
Italy

Huggies
USA

Bugaboo
Netherlands

Graco
USA

MacLaren
United Kingdom

Purina
USA

Whiskas
USA

IAMS
USA

Kent
USA

Friskies
USA

Royal Canin
France

Hill's
USA

Petco
USA

Blue Seal
USA

Bauknecht
Germany

Delta Faucet
USA, 2001
Pentagram: Woody Pirtle

Tornado
France

Moen
USA

Maytag
USA

Smeg
Italy

Paulmann Lighting
Canada

Somfy
France

Jacuzzi
USA

Viking
USA

Electrolux

Electrolux
Sweden, 1962
Carlo L. Vivarelli

 Zalf

 Boffi

Zalf
Italy

Boffi SpA
Italy

 teuco

 Whirlpool

Teuco
Italy

Whirlpool
USA, 2010

 rochebobois

vitra.

Roche Bobois
France

Vitra
Switzerland

 ZANKER

 Míele

Zanker
Germany

Miele
Germany

Frigidaire

Frigidaire
USA, 1955

KitchenAid

KitchenAid
USA

FRIGID△IRE®

Frigidaire
USA, 2009

GAGGENAU

Gaggenau
Germany

Candy
Italy

Sauter

Sauter
France

SPEAKMAN

Speakman
USA

SEVERIN

Severin
Germany

Salton
USA

ZANUSSI

Zanussi
Italy

Noritake

Noritake
China

Moulinex
France

WEST BEND.

West Bend
USA

Broil King

Broil King
Canada

KRUPS

Krups
Germany

Cuisinart

Cuisinart
USA

FARBERWARE

Farberware
USA

magimix

Magimix
France

MR.C✦FFEE

Mr. Coffee
USA

Waring Products
USA

VICTORINOX

Victorinox
Switzerland, 2009

de BUYER
DEPUIS 1830

de Buyer
France

Gerber
USA, 2005

Benchmade
USA

George Foreman
USA

alfi
Germany, 2007
Baumann & Baumann

Buck Knives
USA

Corelle
USA

Wilton
USA

Bunn
Canada

WMF
Germany, 2006
Baumann & Baumann

Zwillings J. A. Henckels
Germany

T-Fal
USA

Tefal
France

CRKT
(Columbia River Knife & Tool)
USA, 1990s

Bodum
Denmark

Bunn-O-Matic
Canada

Frabosk
Italy

Mr. Clean
USA, 1958
Tatham-Laird & Kudner: Ernie Allen

Tide
USA, 2008

Scotts Lawn Products
USA

Glad
USA

Sealy
USA

Cif
France

Serta
USA

Igloo
USA

Harpic
United Kingdom

Spray 'n Wash
USA

Handy Bag
France

Zodiac Marine & Pool
France

SC Johnson Wax
USA

Vileda
Germany

Vizir Ultra
USA

Dirt Devil
USA

Jiffy
Netherlands

Johns Manville
USA

Dawn
USA

Domestos
USA, ca 2002

Clorox
USA, 2010

Lyso + Form
Switzerland

Raid
USA

Lysol
USA, 2010

38

Ajax
USA

Drano
USA

Glade
USA

Glade
USA

Hefty
USA

DAP
USA

Norton Bear-Tex
USA

Simmons
USA, 1998

Weber
USA

Bondo
USA

Velux
Denmark

Softub
USA

Grohe
Germany

Persil

Persil
Germany/United Kingdom

Dixie Cup
USA, 1969
Saul Bass

dyson

Dyson
United Kingdom

Mothers
USA

sikkens

Sikkens
Netherlands

Oreck
USA

Saeco
Italy

Brabantia
Netherlands

Clopay
USA

Brita
Germany

Pritt
Germany

WD-40
USA

Mag-Lite
USA

NORELCO

Norelco
USA

Teleflorist
United Kingdom

Hallmark

Hallmark
USA, 1949
Hallmark: Andrew Szoeke

Teleflora
USA

Hästens

Hästens
Sweden, 2001
Stockholm Design Lab, TEArk

Pattex
Austria

Post-It
USA

Tipp-Ex
Germany

Tesa
Germany, 1990

Eveready
USA

Rubbermaid
USA

Varta
Germany

Talens
Netherlands

UHU
Germany

Energizer
USA

Energizer
USA, 1996

DURACELL

Duracell
USA, 1964
Lippincott

Grandcell
Australia

Rayovac
USA, 2002

Adler
Germany

Tupperware

Tupperware
USA

Scotch

Scotch
USA

John Dickinson

John Dickinson
United Kingdom

Iris Ohyama Inc
Japan

Reckitt Benckiser
United Kingdom, 2009
The Workroom

Ziploc
USA

P&G
USA, 1991
Lipson Alport Glass & Associates

Samsonite
USA

Rimowa
Germany

Tumi
USA

COACH

Coach
USA

KEM Playing Cards
USA

Swiss Army Brands Ltd
Switzerland
Gerard Huerta

Avery
USA, 1975
Saul Bass & Associates

Anthro
USA

Staples
USA

DANKA

Danka
USA

brother

Brother
Japan

OKI

Oki
Japan

X-ACTO
BRAND

X-Acto
USA

ROLODEX

Rolodex
USA

Giroflex
Switzerland

Donau
South Africa

Corporate Express
Netherlands, 1998
DG Design

Mac Papers
USA

Frank Parsons
USA

Esselte
USA

Herman Miller
USA, 1999

KOKUYO

Kokuyo
Japan

Viking
United Kingdom, 2011
Lippincott

okamura

Okamura
Japan

Steelcase

Steelcase
USA

Office DEPOT

Office Depot
USA, 2002

OfficeMax

OfficeMax
USA, 1980s

46

SoftSheen·Carson

Softsheen-Carson
USA

CLAIROL

Clairol
USA

NARS Cosmetics
USA

AVON

Avon
USA

VANTEX

Vantex
USA, 1988

GARNIER

Garnier
France

DECLÉOR
PARIS

Decleor Paris
France

La Prairie
Switzerland

REDKEN
5TH AVENUE NYC

Redken
USA

VICHY
LABORATOIRES

Vichy Laboratoires
France

Kiehl's
USA

Jovan
USA, 1972

Lancôme Paris
France

COVER GIRL

Cover Girl
USA

Shu Uemura Cosmetics
Japan

Revlon Professional
USA

Revlon
USA
Pentagram

Brut
USA

Original Source
United Kingdom

COLGATE-PALMOLIVE

Kimberly-Clark
USA

Colgate-Palmolive
USA

LISTERINE

Gillette

Listerine
USA

Gillette
USA

BAND·AID

Band-Aid
USA, 2006

Zirh International
USA

Le Petit Marseillais
France, 1989

Kuno Moser
Germany

Lady Remington
USA

Old Spice
USA, 2008

Speed Stick
USA

Lady Speed Stick
USA

Kleenex
USA, 2008
Sterling Brands

Renu
USA, 2010
Pentagram: Paula Scher

L'ORÉAL

L'Oréal
France

POND'S

Pond's
United Kingdom/Netherlands

ALMAY

Almay
USA

FABERGÉ

Fabergé
USA

Neutrogena

Neutrogena
USA

Coppertone
USA

AXE

Axe
France

Ban
USA

o.b.
USA

OFF!
USA

Wilkinson Sword
United Kingdom

Lux
United Kingdom

Zest
USA

Vaseline
United Kingdom/Netherlands, 2007

Nivea
Germany, 1993

Remington
USA

Hansaplast
Germany

Colgate
USA

Oral-B
USA

Palmolive
USA

Durex
United Kingdom

52

JESSICA
Jessica
USA

CLINIQUE
Clinique
USA

Oil of Olaz
Germany

The Body Shop
United Kingdom, 2008

Fa Cosmetics
Germany

Geurlain
France

Schwarzkopf
Germany, 1937 (mark)

Herbalife
USA

Wella
Germany, 1993
Klaus Koch Corporate Communications

Framesi
Italy

Crest
USA

Dove
USA, ca 2003

Biotherm
France

Timotei
Sweden

Tampax
USA, 2000s

Trojan
USA

Ivory
USA, 2011
Wieden+Kennedy

Signal
United Kingdom/Netherlands

Curves
USA

URBAN OUTFITTERS

Urban Outifitters
USA

bloomingdale's

Bloomingdale's
USA, 1975
Vignelli Associates

ticketmaster

Ticketmaster
USA

Waldenbooks

Waldenbooks
USA, 1979
Gerard Huerta

BARNES&NOBLE

Barnes & Noble
USA

SELFRIDGES&C°

Selfridges & Co
United Kingdom

BOOKS·A·MILLION

Books-A-Million
USA

The co-operative

The Co-operative
United Kingdom, 2007
Pentagram

ComputerLand

ComputerLand
USA

CurtisMathes

Curtis Mathes
USA

Dia
Spain, 2008

NSB Group
Canada

Safeway
USA, 2005

Designer Depot
Canada, ca 2004

Shoppers Drug Mart
USA

Couche-Tard
Canada, 1999

EuroSpar
Netherlands

Jumbo
Portugal

Sanistal
Denmark

Sobey's
Canada

Quick Chek
USA, 2008
Lippincott

56

Pier 1 imports

Pier 1 Imports Inc
USA

shop at design museum

Design Museum Shop
United Kingdom, 2007
Build

Abu Garcia.

Abu Garcia
Sweden

GRAND UNION

Grand Union
USA, 1980s

MARKS & SPENCER

Marks & Spencer
United Kingdom, 2000

MARKS & SPENCER

Marks & Spencer
United Kingdom, 2007

LINENS·N·THINGS

Linens 'n Things
USA

DELHAIZE GROUP

Delhaize Group
Belgium

BARNEYS NEWYORK

Barneys New York
USA, 1981
Chermayeff & Geismar: Steff Geissbuhler

Christopher & Banks
USA

Do-it-center
USA

Family Fare Supermarkets
USA

Sainsbury's
United Kingdom, 1999
M&C Saatchi

Auchan
France

Fred Meyer
USA, 1999

SuperValu
USA

CompUSA
USA

Levitz
USA

Makro
Netherlands, 2000s

AJ Wright
USA, 2009

Bruno's Supermarkets
USA

True Value
USA, 2006

Argos
United Kingdom, 1999
Interbrand Newell & Sorrell

Shaw's
USA

FIELDS

Fields Department Store
Canada

coles

Coles Supermarkets
Australia, ca 2010

Winn-Dixie
USA, 2006

Surcouf
France

Schnucks
USA

Wegmans
USA, 2008

Burdines

Burdines
USA

ingles

Ingles Markets Inc
USA

Osco Drug

Osco Drug
USA

mervyns

Mervyns
USA

SERVISTAR

ServiStar
USA

FONA

Fona
Denmark

TANDY

Tandy
USA

DAISYTEK

Daisytek
United Arab Emirates

Harrods
United Kingdom, 1967
Minale Tattersfield: Brian Tattersfield

Dan's Foods
USA

macy's

Macy's
USA

HECHT'S

Hecht's
USA

habitat

Habitat
United Kingdom, 2002
Andy Stevens, Paul Neal

WHSmith

WHSmith
United Kingdom, 1990s

Bradlees

Bradlees
USA

L.L.Bean

L.L. Bean
USA
Pentagram

EPA
Switzerland

dm-drogerie markt
Germany

American Stores
Company
USA

Kmart
USA, 1990

S-Mart
Mexico

Albert Heijn
Netherlands, 1965
Allied International
Designers

A&S
USA

ICA
Sweden

Q8
Kuwait, 1986
Wolff Olins

DSW (Designer Shoe
Warehouse)
USA

Rite Aid
USA

ILVA
Denmark

ampm
USA

Cora
Belgium

Hills Department Store
USA

Co-op
Canada

Marui
Japan

Daily's
USA

Ralphs
USA

Eckerd
USA

Argos
United Kingdom, 2010
The Brand Union

Jewel
USA, 1979

Coop Foodstore
United Kingdom

Auto Value Parts Stores
USA

Minol
Germany, 1950s

Factory 2-U
USA

Boron Gas Station
USA

Giant Eagle Inc
USA

JET
USA

Aral
Germany, 1972

Blockbuster
USA
Sandy Cook

Best Buy
USA, 1994

Boots
United Kingdom, 1883
Jesse Boot

Kroger
USA

Fill'er Up
USA

A&P
USA
Lippincott & Margulies

Fay's Drug
USA

Altasfera
Italy

Plymart
USA

Lowe's Home Improvement Warehouse
USA, 1997

Do It Best
USA

Casino Supermarkets
France

Stop & Shop
USA

Elf Service Stations
France

Columbia House
USA

The Mac Store
USA

Rent-2-Own
USA, 1980s

Piggly Wiggly
USA

66

Muji
Japan

Sogo
Japan

KölnTicket
Germany
Helmut Langer

Smart & Final
USA

Carphone Warehouse
United Kingdom

The Phone House
United Kingdom

Perry Sport
Netherlands

Dixons
United Kingdom

El Corte Inglés
Spain

Gamma
Netherlands

Kohl's
USA, 1985

Metro Cash & Carry
Germany

Zeeman
Netherlands

Randalls
USA

Tokyu Hands
Japan

Felissimo
Japan

Saturn
Germany, 1999
KMSTeam: Bruno Marek, Peta Kobrow

Target
USA, 2004

Kaufland
Germany

RadioShack
USA, 1996
Landor Associates

S&H greenpoints
USA

Mammouth
France

Plus
Netherlands

Shinsegae
South Korea

Dillard's
USA

Mitsukoshi
Japan

NorgesGruppen
Norway

Liberty
United Kingdom

Winsor & Newton
United Kingdom

Mr. Jardinage
France

Sanborns
Mexico

Netto
Denmark

Ahold
Netherlands

American Home Shield
USA

Drug Emporium
USA

Douglas
Germany

Wawa
USA

QUELLE.

Quelle
Germany

Marshalls

Marshalls
USA

mothercare

Mothercare
United Kingdom

PRIMARK

Primark
Ireland

Tesco
United Kingdom, 1996

Costco Wholesale
USA, 2005

Real
Germany

Giant-Carlisle
USA

Carrefour
France, 2009
Wolff Olins: Miles Newlyn

Whole Foods Market
USA, 1980s

Willy:s
Sweden

3 Suisses
France

Family Dollar
USA, 2008

Rema 1000
Norway

Conad
(Consorzio Nazionale
Dettaglianti)
Italy

Comet
United Kingdom, 2010
Venturethree

Hemköp
Sweden, 2004
Happy F&B, Forsman & Bodenfors

IKEA
Sweden. 1943

Jewson
United Kingdom

Kesko
Finland

Decathlon
France

Leclerc
France

MMEM
Australia

U
France

Mister Minit
Belgium, 1990s

Darty
France

Lidl
Germany

Autogrill
Italy

7-Eleven
USA, 1960s

Le Bon Marché
France

Celio*
France

Tower Records
USA

Westfield
Australia

Fnac
(Fédération Nationale d'Achats des Cadres)
France

The Home Depot
USA, 1978

74

Food Lion
USA

Mac's Convenience Stores
Canada, 1999

Walmart

Walmart
USA, 2008
Lippincott

WAL★MART

Walmart
USA, 1992
Don Watt

Woolworth
USA

Sav-On Drugs
USA

Marsh Supermarkets
USA

VONS

Vons
USA

BUT
France

Hilo Hattie
USA

Giant Food
USA, 1963

Zellers
Canada, 1975

Giant Food
USA, 2008

Irma
Denmark

Daiei
Japan

The Store
Malaysia

Fuji
Japan

Woolworths
Australia

Spar
Netherlands, 1968
Raymond Loewy

Hering
Brazil

Saks Fifth Avenue
USA, 2007
Pentagram

Saks Fifth Avenue
USA, 1973
Vignelli Associates

Sears
USA, 2004

Sears
USA

JC Penney
USA, 2011
Luke Langhus

Burlington Coat Factory
USA

JC Penney
USA, 1969
Unimark International

Burlington Coat Factory
USA

Polaroid
USA
Paul Giambarba

Fujifilm
Japan, 1992

Polaroid
USA, ca 1976
Paul Giambarba

FUJ**I**FILM

Fujifilm
Japan, 2006

Shinko
USA

xerox

Xerox
USA, 2008
Interbrand

Leica
Germany, 1995
Stankowski & Duschek

Xerox
USA, 1994
Landor Associates

HASSELBLAD

Hasselblad
Sweden

Olympus
Japan

Konica Minolta
Japan, 2003

Lexjet Corporation
USA

AGFA
Belgium, 1984
Schlagheck & Schultes

Kodak
USA, 1971
Peter J. Oestreich

Kodak
USA, 2006
Brand Integration Group

Canon
Japan, 1956

Corbis
USA, 2004
Segura Inc: Carlos Segura

Velbon
Japan

Getty Images
USA, 2000
Pentagram

Photodisc
USA

The Image Bank
USA

Fiery
USA

Advanced Photo System
USA, 1990s

Taniguchi
USA

Nikon
Japan, 2003

Pantone
USA

TAMRON

Tamron
Japan

SIGMA

SIGMA
USA

LEICA

Leica
Germany

YASHICA

Yashica
Japan

Veer
USA

Simple Signs
USA

Pantone Hexachrome
USA

Konica
Japan

Rollei
Germany

Vivitar

Vivitar
USA

PENTAX

Pentax
Japan

Ilford Photo
United Kingdom, ca 1966
Design Research Unit

Imperial Tobacco
United Kingdom

British American Tobacco
United Kingdom

Marlboro
USA

Winston
USA

Dunhill

Dunhill
United Kingdom

SKOAL

Skoal
USA

KOOL

Kool
USA, 1933

Newport

Newport
USA, 1957

Philip Morris International
USA/Switzerland

Gitanes
France

Lucky Strike
USA, 1940
Raymond Loewy

Camel
USA

Kent
United Kingdom

Rizla+
France

Zippo
USA

Zig-Zag
France

John Player Special
United Kingdom

JTI
(Japan Tobacco)
Japan

OCB
France

FASHION
& APPAREL

ACCESSORIES
CLOTHING
EYEWEAR
FASHION LABELS
FOOTWEAR
HAUTE COUTURE
LUXURY
SPORTSWEAR

adidas Sport Heritage
Germany, 1972
Hans Fick

adidas Sport Performance
Germany, 1990
Peter Moore

Umbro
United Kingdom, 1992

Salomon
France

Spalding
USA

Asics Tiger
Japan

JUST DO IT.

Nike
USA, 1971
Carolyn Davidson

Just Do It
USA, 1988
Wieden+Kennedy; Dan Wieden

Nike
USA, 1978

Reebok
United Kingdom, 1986

Speedo
Australia

RBK
United Kingdom, 2006
Arnell Group

Quiksilver
USA

Rossignol
France, 2008

Columbia Sportswear
USA

Diadora
Italy

Reebok
United Kingdom, 2008

Penn
USA

Prince
USA

Wilson
USA

Asics
Japan

Fila
Italy

K2
USA

Fila
Italy

Kappa
Italy, 1969

Canterbury
United Kingdom

Puma
Germany, 1967
Lutz Backes

Mizuno
Japan, 1983

Kiwi
France

Slazenger
United Kingdom

Mammut
Switzerland

Le Coq Sportif
France, 2009

Burton
USA

Fanatic
Germany, 2005
3Deluxe

Alpina Professional Helmets
Germany

Volant
USA

Yamato
Germany

TaylorMade
USA

Butterfly
Germany

Ray Cook Golf
USA

AIRWALK

Airwalk
USA

DAKINE

Dakine
USA

VARIFLEX

Variflex
USA

VETTA

Vetta
USA

PING

PING
USA

Elan
Slovenia

ATOMIC

Atomic Skis
Austria

Nordica
Italy

etnies

Etnies
USA

Body Glove
USA, 1960s
Bill Meistrell

Powell Peralta
USA

Santa Cruz Skateboards
USA, 1973
Jim Phillips

Obey Giant
USA, 1989
Shepard Fairey

Spitfire
USA

Toy Machine
USA

Skate America
USA

David Beckham
United Kingdom, 2004
Eric Vellozzi

C&A
Belgium/Germany, 2011
Saffron Brand Consultants

64
France, 1997

Jonsson
South Africa

Snickers Workwear
Sweden

Aéropostale
USA

Supreme
USA

Wolford
Austria

Wonderbra
USA

Killer Loop
Italy

Under Armour
USA

Jonny Cupcakes Inc
USA

Volcom
USA

Helly Hansen
Norway

National Linen Service
USA

Hanes
USA

Peter Kaiser
Germany

BVD
(Bradley, Voorhees & Day)
USA

VF
USA

Protest Boardwear
Netherlands

Royal Wear
France

Diesel
Italy

Gap
USA, 1986

94

Plan B Skateboards
USA

Haglöfs
Sweden

ZOOMP

Zoomp
Brazil

genetic

Genetic Skateboard
Products
USA

WORTH

Worth
USA

QUEBRAMAR

Quebramar
Portugal

New Era
USA

PIPERLIME

Piperlime
USA, 2006
Pentagram

POLARTEC

Polartec
USA, 1997
Jorgensen Quint

K·WAY

K-Way
Italy

STARTER

Starter
USA

absorba

Absorba
France

Gore-Tex
USA

Windstopper
USA

Petit Bateau
France

Carhartt
USA

Riders
USA

Old Navy
USA

Toyobo
Japan

Bassetti
Italy

The North Clothing
United Kingdom

Roces
Italy

DIM
France

Gas Blue Jeans
Italy

Arrow
USA, ca 1970

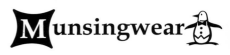

Damart
France

Avirex U.S.A.
USA

Triumph International
Switzerland

Billabong
Australia

Munsingwear
USA

Mooks Clothing Co.
Australia

Powell Peralta
USA

Kenko Ball
Japan

Lanover
Brazil, 1966
Alexandre Wollner

Lee
USA

VANS

Vans
USA, 1960s

DIESEL

Diesel
Italy

Bench.

Bench
United Kingdom

CHEROKEE

Cherokee
USA

Wrangler

Wrangler
USA

OshKosh
B'GOSH

OshKosh B'gosh
USA

極度乾燥(しなさい)
Superdry.

Superdry
United Kingdom, ca 2004

Sloggi
Germany

NEW
MAN

New Man
France, 1969
Raymond Loewy

Salewa
Italy, 1979

Hollister
USA, 2000

Dovre
Norway, 2008
Norges Kreative Fagskole

Ferrioni
Mexico

Roots
Canada

Sorel
Canada

Lonsdale
United Kingdom

Enjoi Skateboarding
USA

Guy Cotten
France

The North Face
USA, 1968

Air Max
USA

Coleman
USA

Peak Performance
Sweden

Toko
Switzerland

Duarig
France, 2000s

Yonex
Japan, 1973

Lycra
USA

WeSC
(We Are the Superlative Conspiracy)
Sweden

IKKS

IKKS Group
France

Yakka

Yakka Apparel Solutions
Australia

L'eggs

L'eggs
USA, 1969
Herb Lubalin Associates:
Roger Ferriter

Patta

Patta
Netherlands

Johnny Loco

Johnny Loco
Netherlands

MacGregor

MacGregor Golf
USA

Globetrotter

Globetrotter
Germany, ca 1985

Titleist

Titleist
USA, 1930s

AIRFiELD

Airfield
Germany

Schöffel

Schöffel
Germany

Rawlings
USA

Champion
USA

Nittaku
Japan

Cordura
USA

Lange
France

Santa Cruz Skateboards
USA

Kobe Sportswear
Canada

REI
USA

Zebco
USA

Rifle
Italy

Head
USA

Marmot
USA

Rip Curl
Australia

O'Neill
USA

Rollerblade
Italy

Alpinestars
Italy

Mistral
Netherlands

Mitre
United Kingdom, 2001

Fischer
Austria

Vaude
Germany

Callaway Golf
USA

The Finals
USA

Descente
Japan, ca 1957

Black Crows
France
Yorgo Tloupas

Lacoste
France, 1930s
Robert George

Chums
USA
Charles S. Anderson Design Co.

Abercrombie & Fitch
USA

Kangol
United Kingdom

Dickies
USA

Tatonka
Germany

Lafuma
France

Fjällräven
Sweden

Jack Wolfskin
Germany, 1980s

Lee Cooper
United Kingdom

Vans "Off the Wall"
USA

Gola
United Kingdom

Erreà
Italy

Foundation Skateboards
USA

Arena
Germany, 1973

Analog Clothing
USA

Vox Footwear
USA

DC Shoes
USA, ca 1993

Dr. Scholl's
United Kingdom

Weinbrenner
USA, 1980s

New Balance
USA

Element Skateboards
USA

Converse
USA

K-Swiss
USA, 1966

Camper
Spain, 1981

Ara
Germany

Bata Shoes
Switzerland

Havaianas
Brazil

BIRKENSTOCK

WOLVERINE

Birkenstock
Germany

Wolverine
USA

Adio Footwear
USA

Teva
USA

Ecco
Denmark

Keds
USA

Darkstar
USA

Shaq (Shaquille O'Neal)
USA, 2005
*Design Ranch: Michelle Sonderegger, Ingred Sidie,
Michelle Martinowicz, Tad Carpenter*

Fallen
USA

LA Gear
USA

New Era
USA

West Coast Choppers
USA

Onitsuka Tiger
Japan

Foot Locker
USA

Air Jordan
USA, 1988
Tinker Hatfield

Rocky
USA

KangaROOS
USA

Superga
Italy, 1999
Brunazzi & Associati: Giovanni Brunazzi

Timberland
USA

Hi-Tec
United Kingdom

Famous Footware
USA, 2005

Oscar de la Renta
USA, 1960s
Oscar de la Renta

agnès b.
France

Paul Smith
United Kingdom
Zena

Pepe Jeans
United Kingdom, 1992

Ben Sherman
United Kingdom

Ben Hogan
USA

H&M
Sweden

Stüssy
USA, 1980
Shawn Stussy

Von Dutch
USA, ca 1950
Kenny Howard (aka Von Dutch)

Superdry
United Kingdom

Paraboot
France

Scandale
France

Playtex
USA

Clarks
United Kingdom

Quiksilver
USA

LANVIN

Lanvin
France

ICEBERG

Iceberg
Italy

CERRUTI

Cerutti
France

MANGO

Mango
Spain, 1984

COLE HAAN

Cole Haan
USA

BANANA REPUBLIC

Banana Republic
USA

RICHEMONT

Richemont
Switzerland

VICTORIA'S SECRET

Victoria's Secret
USA

Dior

Dior
France

GUCCI

Gucci
Italy, 1933
Gucci family

PRADA

Prada
Italy

ZARA

Zara
Spain

BOSS
HUGO BOSS

Hugo Boss
Germany

GUESS
BY MARCIANO

Guess
USA

Armani Exchange
USA, 1991

LVMH
France

Armani Jeans
Italy

Dolce & Gabbana
Italy

Diane von Fürstenberg
USA
Fabien Baron

Ocean Pacific
USA

Calvin Klein
USA

Gucci
Italy, 1933
Gucci family

Yves Saint-Laurent
France, 1963
A. M. Cassandre

Louis Vuitton
France, 1854
Louis Vuitton

Burberry
United Kingdom, 1901

Emporio Armani
Italy

Karl Lagerfeld
Germany

Cheap Monday
Sweden, 2003
Vår

Dunhill London
United Kingdom

Fred Perry
United Kingdom

Hermès
France, 1945
Alfred de Dreux

Montblanc
Germany, 1913

Ralph Lauren
USA

SAMSØE ⏀ SAMSØE

Samsøe & Samsøe
Denmark

Vivienne Westwood
United Kingdom

Versace
Italy

JILSANDER

Jil Sander
Germany

GERRY WEBER

Gerry Weber
Germany, 1990s

TOM FORD

Tom Ford
USA

GF FERRÉ

GF Ferré
Italy
Winkreative

LAGERFELD

Lagerfeld
Germany

STEFANEL

Stefanel
Italy

ESCADA

Escada
Germany

KOOKAÏ

Kookaï
France, 1983

LALIQUE

Lalique
France

fcuk

fcuk
United Kingdom
TBWA: Trevor Beattie

DKNY

Donna Karan New York
USA, 1989
Arnell Group: Peter Arnell

FENDI

Fendi
Italy

KENZO

Kenzo
France

ESPRIT

Esprit
USA, 1979
John Casado

Polo Jeans Company
USA

Burberry
United Kingdom

Tommy Hilfiger
USA

UNITED COLORS
OF BENETTON.

United Colors of Benetton
Italy, 1995
Vignelli Associates

Uniqlo
Japan, 2007
Kashiwa Sato

Levi's
USA

S I S L E Y

Sisley
Italy, 1996

STELL/MCC/RTNEY

Stella McCartney
United Kingdom
Winkreative

VIDAL SASSOON

Vidal Sassoon
United Kingdom

MARC JACOBS

Marc Jacobs
USA

Calvin Klein

Calvin Klein
USA

liz claiborne

Liz Claiborne
USA

DSQUARED²

Dsquared2
Italy, 1998
Giovanni Bianco Studio 65

GIVENCHY

Givenchy
France

GIANNI VERSACE

Gianni Versace
Italy

ZADIG & VOLTAIRE

Zadig & Voltaire
France

GIORGIO ARMANI

Giorgio Armani
Italy

CHANEL

Chanel
France

Jean Paul Gautier
(website)
France

Tom Tailor
Germany

VAN HEUSEN

Van Heusen
USA

ANNE KLEIN

Anne Klein
USA

diana ferrari

Diana Ferrari
Australia

Miu Miu
Italy

FINANCE

BANKING
CREDIT CARDS
FINANCIAL SERVICES
FOREIGN EXCHANGE
INVESTMENT
INSURANCE
PAYMENT SYSTEMS
STOCK EXCHANGES

Irwin Financial
USA, 1990
Paul Rand

Commonwealth Bank
Australia

Nishi-Nippon Bank
Japan

Guoco Group
China

Volksbank
Austria

Transamerica
USA

**Sparkassen-
Finanzgruppe**
Germany

Suomi Mutual
Finland

First Interstate Bank
USA

Canada Trust
Canada

Bank of Beijing
China

Banco del Pacifico
Ecuador, 1972
Versus: Peter Mussfeldt

**Golden West
Financial Corporation**
USA

The Global Fund
Switzerland

American Express
USA, 1975
Lippincott

Visa
USA, 1993

New York Life
USA, 1964
*Lippincott & Margulies:
Raphael Boguslav*

The Bank of New York
USA

Goldman Sachs
USA

Union Bank of California
USA

AXA
France

TD (Toronto-
Dominion Bank)
Canada, 1969

Ace Group
Switzerland
Interbrand

Nationwide
USA

Harris Bank
USA

World Bank
USA

East West Bancorp
USA

Fuji Bank
Japan

Delta Card
USA

CIC (Crédit Industriel
et Commercial)
France

OMC Card
Japan

Saxo Bank
Denmark

AIG (American
International Group)
USA

DC Card
Japan

Great Western Bank
USA

CIB (Commercial
International Bank)
Egypt

Chubb
USA, 1968
Raymond Loewy

Plus
USA

JCB Brand Partner
Japan

MasterCard
USA, 1997
Interbrand

Electronic Cash (EC)
Germany

MasterCard
USA, 2016
Pentagram

ICBC
(Industrial and Commercial Bank of China)
China

CTIC
(Chicago Title Insurance Company)
USA

Lehman Brothers
USA

WARBURG PINCUS

Warburg Pincus
USA

charles SCHWAB

Charles Schwab
USA

Morgan Stanley

Morgan Stanley
USA, 2001
Landor Associates

Standard & Poor's
USA
Lippincott

Bear Stearns
USA

ABN·AMRO

ABN AMRO
Netherlands, 1991
Landor Associates

 VeriFone

VeriFone
USA

 NATIXIS

Natixis
France

NatWest

NatWest
United Kingdom, 2003
The Partners

NISSAY

Nissay
Japan

MetLife

MetLife
USA

H&R BLOCK

H&R Block
USA, 2000

 Huntington

Huntington
USA, 2010

 KB BANKI

KB Banki
Iceland

 WaMu

Washington Mutual
USA

Frost Bank
USA

Prudential Insurance Company of America
USA, 1990
Siegel+Gale

Northern Trust
USA

Skandia
Sweden

Scotiabank
Canada

Shinsei Bank
Japan

State Farm
USA

Pohjola
Finland

Dresdner Bank
Germany, 2005
Claus Koch

Lloyds TSB
United Kingdom

Central Bank
USA

Barclaycard
United Kingdom, 2009
The Brand Union

Banamex
Mexico
Lippincott

Abbey
United Kingdom, 2005

Salling Bank
Denmark

Sanwa Bank
Japan

Koçbank
Turkey

Mapfre
Spain

First Data
USA, 2008
VSA Partners

Tokio Marine Nichido
Japan

TOKYO
STOCK EXCHANGE

Tokyo Stock Exchange
Japan

First Citizens Bank
USA

New York Stock Exchange

NYSE
(New York Stock Exchange)
USA, 2000
Landor Associates

TSX
(Toronto Stock Exchange)
Canada

Jones Lang LaSalle
USA

London Stock Exchange
United Kingdom

Janus Capital
USA, 2003
Templin Brink Design: Joel Templin, Gaby Brink

Liberty Mutual
USA

Rand Merchant Bank
South Africa

UBS
Switzerland, 1998
Interbrand Zintzmeyer & Lux

Postbank
Netherlands

Reliance Life Insurance
India

Firstar Bank
USA

JSF
Japan

Erie Insurance
USA

Nemi Forsikring
Norway

Freddie Mac
USA

First Horizon
USA

NASDAQ

NASDAQ
USA

DOWJONES

Dow Jones
USA, 1997
Belk Mignogna Associates

EUROCARD

Eurocard
Belgium

DnB NOR

DnB NOR
Norway, 2003
Scandinavian Design Group

EQUIFAX

Equifax
USA

AKBANK

Akbank
Turkey

MORE TH>N

More Th>n
United Kingdom, 2000
Johnson Banks

.ıDekaBank

DekaBank
Germany

CASH STATION

Cash Station
USA

UnionCentral

Union Central
USA

Visa
USA, 2006
Greg Silveria, Visa International Brand Management

Citibank
USA, 1999
Pentagram: Paula Scher

BBVA

BBVA
Spain

PayPal
USA
Chad Hurley

**CREDIT
SUISSE**

Credit Suisse
Switzerland, 1997
Wolff Olins

DKV
(Deutsche Krankenversicherung)
Germany, 2003
MetaDesign

GEICO

Geico Direct
USA

NOMURA

Nomura
Japan

GMAC (General
Motors Acceptance
Corporation)
USA

UMB

UMB Financial
Corporation
USA

ABP
Netherlands

Ætna

Aetna
USA

BankBoston
USA

Barclays
United Kingdom, 2004
Williams Murray Hamm

Fannie Mae
USA

Merrill Lynch
USA, 1974
King Casey

Transamerica
USA

Manulife Financial Corporation
Canada

Fideuram Vita
Italy

Federal Reserve Bank of Boston
USA

U.S. Bank
USA

Crédit Agricole
France, 1987

Dow Jones Interactive
USA

Diners Club
USA

Kagawa Bank
Japan

UniCredit Group
Italy

BNP Paribas
France

Bank of Montreal/Banque de Montréal
Canada, 1967
Stewart & Morrison: Hans Kleefeld

Irwin Financial
USA, 1999
Chermayeff & Geismar: Steff Geissbuhler

Nidwaldner Kantonalbank
Switzerland

Aichi Bank
Japan

Taiwan Business Bank
Taiwan

Rabobank
Netherlands, 2010
Edenspiekermann

Bank of the West
USA

Gras Savoye
France

Taiwan Cooperative Bank
Taiwan

Massachusetts Credit Union League
USA

Crédit Mutuel
France

Great Eastern Group
Singapore/Malaysia

Abbey National
United Kingdom, 2001

AMERICA'S
CREDIT UNIONS

America's Credit Unions
USA, 1999

AMERICAN
CENTURY

American Century Investments
USA

Adelaide Bank
Australia

ComfortMind
Canada

Fieldstone Mortgage Company
USA

American Family Insurance
USA

Star Networks
USA

Guide One Insurance
USA

136

HSBC
United Kingdom, 1999
Henry Steiner

Citibank
USA, 1970s
*Anspach Grossman Enterprise:
Gene Grossman*

Chase
USA, 2006
Sandstrom Design

Allianz
Germany, 1999
Claus Koch

Skandia
Sweden, 2008

Helvetia
Switzerland, 2006

Travelers Insurance
USA

ING
Netherlands, 1991

VGH
Germany

UBI Banca
Italy, 2007

Bank of America
USA, 1998
Enterprise IG

Credit Suisse
Switzerland, 2005
Enterprise IG

Deutsche Bank
Germany, 1974
Stankowski & Duschek:
Anton Stankowski

Commerzbank
Germany, 2009
MetaDesign

Roskilde Bank
Denmark

Higashi-Nippon Bank
Japan

DenizBank
Turkey

BNI
(Bahrain National Insurance)
Bahrain

Wiener Städtische
Austria

Standard Chartered Bank
United Kingdom

Coutts & Co
United Kingdom

Nationale Bank van België
(National Bank of Belgium)
Belgium

NYCE
(New York Cash Exchange)
USA, 1984
Siegel+Gale

Navy Federal
USA

Okasan Securities
Japan, 1991
Paul Rand

Orix
Japan

Philippine Stock
Exchange
Philippines

National Leasing
Canada

Norwich Union
United Kingdom

Halifax
United Kingdom, 1980s

BANK
GESELLSCHAFT
BERLIN

Bankgesellschaft Berlin
Germany

The Exchange
Canada/USA, 1970s

XL
United Kingdom, 2011
Venturethree

De Nederlandsche Bank
Netherlands

De Nederlandsche Bank
Netherlands

Danamon
Indonesia, 2006
BD+A Design

FirstMerit
USA

栃木銀行

Tochigi Bank
Japan

Aegon
Netherlands

Deutsche Börse
Germany, 1995
Stankowski & Duschek

Santander
Spain
Landor Associates

Postbank
Germany

Tryg
Denmark

Dexia
Belgium

Moneo
France

Standard Bank
South Africa

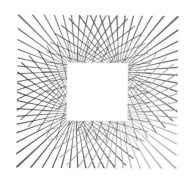

The Bank of New York
USA, 2005
Lippincott Mercer

Wells Fargo
USA

Western Union
USA

Sümerbank
Turkey

Unibanco
Brazil

Groupama
France

Nationwide Building Society
United Kingdom, 1994

American Republic Insurance Company
USA, 1964
Chermayeff & Geismar

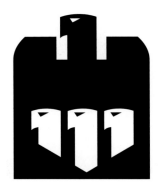

Allianz
Germany, 1923
Karl Schulpig

Federated Investors
USA

FleetBoston Financial
USA

First American Real Estate
USA

Independent Bank
USA

Barclays
United Kingdom, 1981
John York

FIDELITY NATIONAL

Fidelity Bank
USA

Fidelity Bank
USA

The Hartford
USA

Unibank
Denmark

LORD ABBETT

Lord Abbett
USA

Banque Royale

Banque Royale
Canada

BANK PEKAO SA

Bank Pekao
Poland, 1997
Mars & Venus

Guardian
Insurance

Guardian Insurance
USA

TOKIO MARINE

Mitsui Sumitomo Insurance

Tokio Marine Nichido
Japan

Mitsui Sumitomo
Japan

Wachovia
USA

Aviva
United Kingdom, 2001
Corporate Edge

Porto Seguro
Brazil

United Fire Group
USA

MUFG

Mitsubishi UFJ Financial Group
Japan

Bank of China
China

Allstate

Allstate Insurance
USA

ZURICH

Zurich
Switzerland

Scottish Equitable

Scottish Equitable
United Kingdom

TICOR TITLE

Ticor Title
USA

HANCOCK BANK

Hancock Bank
USA

Guaranty Bank
AND TRUST COMPANY

Guaranty Bank and Trust Company
USA

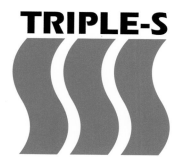

TRIPLE-S

Triple-S
Puerto Rico

MERCURY

Mercury Insurance Group
USA

KeyBank
USA

Refco
USA

Swiss Life
Switzerland, 2006
MetaDesign

Taishin Bank
Taiwan, 1992

TK Techniker
Krankenkasse
Germany, 1987

Shinkin Central Bank
(SCB)
Japan

Nipponkoa Insurance
Japan

Keiyo Bank
Japan

Castle Alternative Invest
Switzerland

Market System
Brazil

SouthTrust Bank
USA

Mackenzie Financial
Canada

Assurant
USA, 2004
Carbone Smolan Agency

Ageas
United Kingdom

**First Federal Bank
of California**
USA

Athens First
USA

Fidelity Investments
USA

Commerzbank
Germany

HFC (Household Finance Corporation)
USA

DAS
United Kingdom

FOOD & DRINK

BEVERAGES
CANDIES
CHOCOLATE
FAST FOOD
FOOD PRODUCTS
ICE CREAM
RESTAURANTS & BARS
SAVORY FOODS
SNACKS
SWEETS
PACKAGED FOODS
WINES, BEERS & SPIRITS

Coca-Cola
USA, 2007
Turner Duckworth

Coca-Cola
USA, 1969
Lippincott & Margulies

Diet Coke
USA, 2007

Coca-Cola
USA, 1941
Frank M. Robinson

Pepsi-Cola
USA, 1940

Pepsi
USA, 2008
Arnell Group

Pepsi
USA, 2003

Cherry Coke
USA

Milca Soda Roja
Nicaragua

Effect Energy Drink
Germany

Mountain Dew
USA, 2005

7 Up (USA)
USA

Gatorade
USA, 1991

7 Up (International)
USA, 2011
TracyLocke

Dairy Crest
United Kingdom

Snapple
USA, 2000

Diet Snapple
USA, 2000

Dr Pepper
USA, 1968

Diet Dr Pepper
USA, ca 1987

Canada Dry
USA, 2009

Sprite
USA, 2009

Schweppes
United Kingdom

Perrier
France

Orangina
Japan/USA, 2010

Squirt
USA, ca 2002

Orangina
Japan/USA, 2007

Sunkist
USA, 1990s

Sunkist
USA, 2010

Fanta
USA, 1980

Fanta
USA, 1980s

Fanta
USA, 2000

Fanta
USA, 2009
Office

Mini Stop
Japan

Lipton Ice Tea
United Kingdom/
Netherlands

Tchibo
Germany

Illy
Italy, 1996
James Rosenquist

Dark Dog
Austria, ca 2001

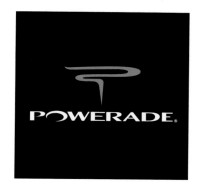

Powerade
USA

Sprite
USA, 1994

Nestlé Crunch
Switzerland

Green Canteen
USA, 2008
Pentagram

Afri Cola
Germany

Long John Silver's
USA, 2011

The Greene Turtle
USA

Klondike
USA

The Schwan
Food Company
USA

Rigas piena kombinats
Latvia

Shark Energy Drink
Thailand

Birds Eye
United Kingdom, 1940s

Lete
Italy

Franck Kava
Croatia

Vittel
France

Ferrarelle
Italy

Sara Lee
USA

Crocodille
Czech Republic

Granini
Germany

Maltesers
USA

Canderel
USA
Team Créatif

Müller
Germany

Campbell's
USA, ca 1900

Jacobs
Germany

Lavazza
Italy, 1992

Nescafé
Switzerland

albi

Albi
Germany

GLACÉAU

Glacéau
USA

BONAQUA

Bonaqua
USA

Up & Go
Australia

AJINOMOTO

Ajinomoto
Japan, 1999

AdeS
Brazil

Tropicana

Tropicana
USA

Innocent
United Kingdom, 1999
Gravy (aka David Streek), Deepend

Dunkin' Donuts
USA, 2002

Dunkin' Donuts
USA, 2006

Van Houten
Sweden

Sweet'n Low
USA, 1950s

Baskin-Robbins
USA, 1994
Lippincott & Margulies

ConAgra Foods
USA, 2009
Bailey Lauerman

Ülker
Turkey

Meiji
Japan, 1971
Yusaku Kamekura

158

Melitta
Germany

Walter
USA

Culligan
USA

Friendly's
USA

Cadbury
United Kingdom

Chocolat Poulain
France

Chick-fil-A
USA, 1964
Louie Floyd Giglio Jr

おいしさと健康

Glico
Japan, 1992

Frisch's
USA

Maggi
Switzerland

Toblerone
Switzerland, 1908 (wordmark)

Volvic
France

Tirol Milch
Austria

Rivella
Switzerland, 2007

Evian
France

160

Diplom-Is
(Eskimonika)
Norway

SPA
Belgium

Chiquita
USA, ca 1944
Dik Browne

Farmer John
USA

DANONE
Danone
France, 1994

QUAKER
Quaker Oats
USA, 2010
Wallace Church

Voortman
Voortman
Canada

Carl's Jr.
USA, 1997

Café de Colombia
Colombia, ca 1981
DDB Worldwide

Nestlé
Switzerland

Big Boy
USA
Ben Washam

Little Chef
United Kingdom
Venturethree

Utz
USA

Five Chefs
Russia

Lindt
Switzerland

Godiva Chocolatier
Belgium, 1993
Pentagram: Michael Bierut

After Eight
United Kingdom

Sarotti
Germany, 2004
Peter Schmidt Group

Leonidas Pralines
Belgium

Rita's
USA

Langnese
Germany, 1960s

Ritz Crackers
USA

Langnese
Germany

Miko
France, 1980s

Cornetto
United Kingdom, 2018
Design Bridge

164

Haribo Boy
Germany

Ronald McDonald
USA, ca 1967
Barry Klein

M&M's
USA, 1972

Pringles
USA

Pringles
USA, 1996

Blue Band
United Kingdom/Netherlands

Taco Bell
USA, 1994

Danish Crown
Denmark

Westbrae Natural
USA

Magnum
United Kingdom, 2006

Nespresso
Switzerland

Maestrani Swiss Chocolate
Switzerland, 1990

S. Pellegrino
Italy, 1999
Minale Tattersfield

Mövenpick
Switzerland, 1999
Conran Design Group

M&M's
USA

Dove
USA

Carambar
France

Blimpie
USA, 2005

Tic Tac
Italy

Breyers
USA

Milky Way
USA

Skittles
USA

Rollitos
USA

Chi-Chi's
USA

Crem Helado
Colombia

Chupa Chups
Spain, 1969
Salvador Dalí

HERSHEY'S

Hershey's
USA

WRIGLEY'S

Wrigley's
USA

SMINT.

Smint
Spain

EAT.

EAT.
United Kingdom, 2002
Pentagram

MARS

Mars
USA

MAILLE

Maille
France

mentos

Mentos
Netherlands

FERRERO

Ferrero
Italy

Snapple

Snapple
USA, 2008
CBX

Cheerios

Cheerios
USA

Fisherman's Friend
United Kingdom

AB InBev
Belgium, 2008
FutureBrand

Côte d'Or
Belgium

Quaker Oats
USA, 1957
Haddon Sundblom

Quaker Oats
USA, 1971
Saul Bass

Hollywood Chewing Gum
France

Stimorol
Denmark

Snickers
USA, 2003

Amora
France

Puget
France

Act II
USA

Malaco
Sweden, 2000s

St. Ivel
United Kingdom

The Cheesecake Factory
USA

Nathan's Famous
USA

Entenmann's
USA

Cailler of Switzerland
Switzerland

Upper Crust
United Kingdom

Wiener's der Kaffee
Germany, 1985

Whitman's
USA

Bennigan's
USA, 1990s

Kettle Chips
USA

Doritos
USA, 2000

Doritos
USA, 1990s

Doritos
USA, 1964

Doritos
USA, 1980s

Lay's
USA, 2003

Frito Lay
USA, 1997
Landor Associates

Quick meals
Russia
Alexey Shelepov

Vienna Beef
USA

Gatorade
USA, 2009

General Mills
USA, 2001

Schwartz
Canada

Sanford Limited
New Zealand

Uncle Ben's
USA

Golden Toast
Germany

Denny's
USA

Buitoni
Italy

Thomy
Switzerland

Hahne
Germany

PowerBar
USA

Fonzies
Italy

Weston
Canada

Marmite
United Kingdom

Mafka
Russia

Oroweat
USA

Keebler
USA
Raphael Boguslav

Krispy Kreme
USA, 1937
Benny Dinkins

Kellogg's
USA, 1906
Will Keith Kellogg

Tofutti
USA

Libby's
USA

La Laitière
France

Knorr
United Kingdom/Netherlands

Milka
Switzerland

French's
USA, 1921

Betty Crocker
USA, 1950s
Lippincott

Oreo
USA, 1987

Oreo
USA, 2004

Kix
USA

Domino Sugar
USA

Cheetos
USA, 2000s

Chips Ahoy!
USA

SunChips
USA, 1991

Monte
Germany

Bisquick
USA, 2004

Brill
USA

Jell-O
USA, 2006

Cracker Jack
USA

Dr Pepper
USA, 1997

Tartex
Germany

Saputo
Canada

HARIBO

Haribo
Germany

Pago
Germany

Bremykt
Norway

Mars
United Kingdom

Trix
USA

Del Valle
USA

Looza
Belgium

LeHA
Germany

Orange Julius
USA

Planters
USA

Red Bull
Thailand/Austria

La vache qui rit
France, 1990s

Kerrygold
Ireland, 1980
Fanstone Group

Alpura
Mexico

Sirloin Stockade
USA

Pillsbury Doughboy
USA, 1965
Leo Burnett: Rudy Perz, Martin Nodell

Mamie Nova
France

Starbucks
USA, 2011
Lippincott, Starbucks in-house design team

Batavo
Brazil

nutella

Nutella
Italy

Kinder

Kinder
Germany, 1967

vitaminwater

Vitaminwater
USA

Mueller's

Mueller's
USA

Slim·Fast!

Slim-Fast
USA

Twinkie

Twinkie
USA

Mounds

Mounds
USA

Almond Joy

Almond Joy
USA

Leprino Foods
USA

CPC International
(Corn Products International)
USA

Luckyfish
USA, 2007
Pentagram

Picard
France

Tine
Norway

Friesland Coberco Dairy Foods
Netherlands

Raisio Group
Finland

Gayelord Hauser
USA

Lowe's Foods
USA

Domino's Pizza
USA, 1997

Jack in the Box
USA, 1980

Dairy Queen (DQ)
USA, 2001

Dairy Queen (DQ)
USA, 1960

Jack in the Box
USA, 2009
Duffy & Partners

Gold Star Chili
USA

Dairy Queen
USA, 2007

Herta
Germany

Lieken Urkorn
Germany

Frito Lay
USA, ca 1985

TNT Energy Drink
Brazil

Subway
USA, 2002

Dentyne
USA

Leerdammer
Netherlands

Trappey's
USA

Van Camp's
USA

Dasani
USA

Life Savers
USA, 1999

Kool-Aid
USA

Kit Kat
USA

Dr. Oetker
Germany

Nestlé
Switzerland

Kraft
USA

Danone
France

Galbani
Italy

Dannon
USA

Gadoua
Canada

Nalley Foods
USA

Nabisco
USA
Bernhardt Fudyma Design Group

Findus
Sweden, 2001

Slim-Fast
USA, 1970s

Verkade
Netherlands

Tim Hortons
Canada

Wander
Switzerland

Royco
South Africa

Peter Paul
USA

Subway
USA, 1968

Starbucks
USA
Heckler Associates: Terry Heckler

Double Coffee
Latvia, 2002

Einstein Bros. Bagels
USA, ca 1995

Panda Express
USA

Legal Sea Foods
USA

Arm & Hammer
USA

The Coffee Bean
& Tea Leaf
USA

Planet Hollywood
USA

Hard Rock Café
USA, 1971
Alan Aldridge

Clearly Canadian
Canada

Kungsörnen
Sweden, 2001

Randy's Donuts
USA, 1950

CoffeeCompany
Netherlands

Milk
Canada

Céréal
France

192

Fritos
USA, 2004

Crisco
USA

Culver's
USA

Post
USA

Burger King
USA, 1999
Sterling Brands

Burger King
USA, 1994

Hungry Jack's
Australia

The Green Burrito
USA

Wimpy
United Kingdom, 1960s

Hoover
USA, ca 1940
Raymond Loewy

Tabasco
USA

Vichy Pastilles
France

Yoplait
France

Philadelphia Cream Cheese
USA, 2008

V8 Vegetable Juice
USA

XXX Energy Drink
Netherlands

Océ
Netherlands, 1982
Baer Cornet

Pillsbury
USA

McDonald's
USA, 1968

McDonald's
USA, 1962
Jim Schindler

McDonald's
USA, 2003
Heye & Partner

McDonald's Drive Thru
USA

Baskin-Robbins
USA, 2006

Dolly Madison Bakery
USA

Lipton
United Kingdom/Netherlands, ca 1890

Mission
USA

El Pollo Loco
USA, 1975

Del Monte Foods
USA, 1990

Wendy's
USA, 1969

T.G.I. Friday's
USA, 1965

KFC
USA, 1997
Landor Associates

White Castle
USA, 2003

Johnny's Pizza House
USA

Lee's Sandwiches
USA

Salisbury House
Canada

Pret A Manger
United Kingdom, ca 1986

Ritter Sport
Germany

Häagen-Dazs
USA

Godfather's Pizza
USA

Outback Steakhouse
USA

ABCO Foods
USA

I Can't Believe It's Yogurt (ICBIY)
USA

Ivar's
USA

Unifrutti
Chile, 1982
Alex Gonzales

Quick
France

Dole
USA, 1986
Landor Associates

Ore-Ida
USA

Whataburger
USA, 1967

Wienerschnitzel
USA, 1978
Saul Bass

Pizza Hut
USA, 1967
Lippincott & Margulies

Pizza Hut
USA, 1999

Flap Jack Restaurants
USA

Cottee's
Australia

Iglo
Belgium, 1983

Don Smallgoods
Australia

Fat Tuesday
USA

K-Salat
Denmark, 2001

Del Taco
USA, 1992

Humpty Dumpty
Canada

Wonder Bread
USA

Green Burrito
USA

In-N-Out Burger
USA

Ball Park
USA

Triple O's
Canada

Skippy
USA

Tim Hortons
Canada

Harry's
France

Rally's
USA

Lustucru
France

202

Jack Daniel's
USA

William Lawson's
United Kingdom

Guinness
Ireland, 2005

Schmidt
USA

Polar Ice Vodka
Canada

Michelob
USA

Johnnie Walker
United Kingdom, 1908
Tom Browne

Laurent-Perrier
France

Dom Pérignon
France

Gautier Cognac
France

Sol
Netherlands

Red Stripe
Jamaica

CORGOŇ

Corgon
Slovakia

SKOL

Skol
Brazil

Asahi Breweries
Japan

Labatt's

Labatt's
Canada

Coors

Coors
Canada

Grolsch
Netherlands

PAULANER

LÖWENBRÄU

Paulaner
Germany

Löwenbräu
Germany

Dewar's

FOSTER'S
GROUP LTD

Dewar's
United Kingdom

Foster's Group
Australia, 2011

Budweiser
USA, 2011

FONDÉ EN 1743

MOËT & CHANDON

CHAMPAGNE

Moët & Chandon
France

Tuborg Beer
Denmark

König Pilsener
Germany

Sibirskaya Korona
Russia

Thor
Denmark

Miller
USA
Brian Collins

Bud
USA

SABMiller
United Kingdom

Bud Light
USA

Super Bock
Portugal

Coopers Brewery
Australia

Labatt Blue
Canada

Viru Valge
Estonia

Victoria Bitter (VB)
Australia

Foster's
Australia

William Grant's
United Kingdom

Pop
China

Pernod Ricard
France

Corona Extra
Mexico

Labatt Ice
Canada

Clan Campbell
United Kingdom

Bacardi
Cuba, ca 1997

Anheuser-Busch
USA

Salitos Tequila
Panama

Pabst Brewing Company
USA

James Squire
Australia

Grasshöpper
Canada

Polar Pilsen
Venezuela

Boréale
Canada

Cerveza Zulia
Venezuela

Tiger Beer
Singapore

Frïs Vodka
Denmark

Diageo
United Kingdom, 1997
Wolff Olins

V&S

V&S (Vin & Spirit)
Sweden

J&B
United Kingdom

Jupiler
Belgium

Karlsberg
Germany

Sagres Cerveja
Portugal

Tecate
Mexico

Lone Star
USA

XX Special Lager
Mexico

Jim Beam
USA

Malibu Rum
Barbados

Pelforth
France

Murphy's Irish Stout
Ireland

Gordon's Gin
United Kingdom

OB Lager
South Korea

Smirnoff
Russia

Smirnoff
Russia

Offley Porto
Portugal

Brains
United Kingdom

Guinness
Ireland, 1997

Veuve Clicquot Ponsardin
France

Baileys Irish Cream
Ireland

Cointreau
France

Danzka Vodka
Denmark

Campari
Italy

Cinzano
Italy

Ricard
France

José Cuervo
Mexico

Drambuie
United Kingdom

Martini
Italy, 1929

Coors Light
Canada

Stoli Razberi
Russia

Budweiser Budvar Brewery
Czech Republic

Carlsberg
Denmark, 2011
Office

Coopers Brewery
Australia

Stroh's
USA

Staropramen
Czech Republic

Radeberger
Germany

Gaffel Kölsch

Gaffel Kölsch
Germany

ABSOLUT
Country of Sweden
VODKA

Absolut Vodka
Sweden

Seagram's

Seagram's
Canada

Oro Azul Tequila
Mexico

★ **Heineken**®

Heineken
Netherlands, 1999
Edenspiekermann

 *Frankenheim*

Frankenheim
Germany

PORTO CRUZ

Porto Cruz
Portugal

DAVIDOFF
COGNAC

Davidoff Cognac
Switzerland

GOVERNMENT & INSTITUTIONS

ASSOCIATIONS
CHURCHES
CITIES & COUNTRIES
CLUBS & SPORTS CLUBS
FOUNDATIONS
INSTITUTIONS
MUSEUMS
ORGANIZATIONS
POLITICAL PARTIES
SCHOOLS & COLLEGES
UNIVERSITIES

I Teach NYC
USA, 2008
Pentagram

Live Aid
United Kingdom, 1985
Bob Geldof, Steve Maher

**Environmental
Choice Program**
Canada

**A Special Wish
Foundation**
USA

**IFAW (International
Fund for Animal Welfare)**
Canada

Iles de Paix
Belgium

**RICS (Royal Institution
of Chartered Surveyors)**
United Kingdom

WWF
Switzerland, 2000
Samenwerkende Ontwerpers

Little Red Door
USA, 2004
Essex Two

The Salvation Army
United Kingdom, ca 1915

**FEAD (European Federation of Waste
Management and Environmental Services)**
Belgium
Helmut Langer

**UNDP
(United Nations Development Programme)**
USA

Swiss Paraplegics Foundation
Switzerland

Swiss Paraplegic Centre
Switzerland

Art Institute of Chicago
USA, 2008
Pentagram: Abbott Miller

The Glass House
(The Philip Johnson Glass House)
USA, 2008
Pentagram

IEA (Institute of
Economic Affairs)
United Kingdom

CIPEC (Canadian
Industry Program for
Energy Conservation)
Canada

Film Council
United Kingdom

Fondation de France
France

AIGA
(American Institute of Graphic Arts)
USA

222

Amnesty International
United Kingdom, 1961
Diana Redhouse

American Film Institute (AFI)
USA, 1968

Steel Recycling Institute
USA

D&AD (Design & Art Direction)
United Kingdom, 2006
Rose

Red Cross
Switzerland, 1863
*Guillaume-Henri Dufour,
Henry Dunant, Louis Appia*

Vårdförbundet
Sweden, 1999
Stockholm Design Lab

Colegio de Arquitectos
Venezuela, 1977
Ílvaro Sotillo

**D&AD
(Design & Art Direction)**
United Kingdom, 1962
Alan Fletcher

Deutsches Zentrum
Ecuador, 2007
Helou Design

Children's Miracle Network
USA

Dubai Cares
United Arab Emirates

Sunflower Children
USA

United Way of America
USA, 2004
FutureBrand: David Weinberger

Christian Aid
United Kingdom, 2006
johnson banks

CINEMA FOR PEACE

Cinema for Peace Foundation
Germany

LEGAMBIENTE

Legambiente
Italy

Goodwill Industries International
USA, 1968
Joseph Selame

British Waterways
United Kingdom, 2004
Design Bridge

Instituto Terra e Memória
Portugal

FSC (Forest
Stewardship Council)
Germany

PEFC (Programme for
the Endorsement
of Forest Certification)
Switzerland

National Trust
United Kingdom, 1980s
David Gentleman

4-H
USA
Oscar Herman Benson

Green Chemistry
Challenge
USA, 1990s

National Institutes
of Health (NIH)
USA, 1976

TeleFood
Italy, ca 1997

Corrugated Recycles
USA

UNICEF
USA

World Health Organization
(WHO)
Switzerland

United Nations
(UN)
USA, 1946
Oliver Lincoln Lundquist, Donal McLaughlin

National Library of Australia
Australia

UNESCO
France

CMAS (Confédération Mondiale
des Activités Subaquatiques)
Italy

Royal Life Saving Society
Australia

Fraternal Order of Eagles International
USA

Boy Scouts of America
USA

UMWA (United Mine
Workers of America)
USA

Optimist International
USA

Canadian
Paediatric Society
Canada

Credit Union
USA

POW-MIA
(Prisoners of War/Missing in Action)
USA
William Graham Wilkin III

Stop Aids Now!
Netherlands, 2000

Action for children
United Kingdom

Friends of the Earth
USA, 2001

Stena
Sweden

IEEE
USA, 1963

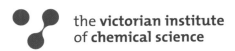

The Victorian Institute of Chemical Science
Australia, 2006
Dale Harris

Action for Blind People
United Kingdom

Goethe-Institut
Germany

Smithsonian
USA, 1997
Chermayeff & Geismar

Centrepoint
United Kingdom

Global Reporting Initative
Netherlands

British Council
United Kingdom

Volunteers of America
USA

American Red Cross
USA

Creative Commons
USA
Creative Commons

Mind
United Kingdom, 2004
Glazer

Greenpeace
Netherlands

Actionaid
South Africa, 2003
CDT

read·ing mat·ters

Reading Matters
United Kingdom
Brahm

Shelter

Shelter
United Kingdom, 2003
johnson banks

Feed Nova Scotia
United Kingdom

SETI Institute
(Search for Extra Terrestrial Intelligence)
USA, 1998
Turner Duckworth

Deutsche Nationalbibliothek
Germany, 2007
Claus Koch

230

National Geographic
USA
Chermayeff & Geismar

Thames Valley Housing
United Kingdom

DGOF (Deutsche Gesellschaft
für Online-Forschung)
Germany, 2007
Enorm

Pen Club Venezuela
Venezuela, 2009
Ariel Pintos

Fraunhofer Society
Germany, 2009

ACORN
(Association of Community
Organizations for Reform Now)
USA

NAHB
(National Association of Home Builders)
USA

DGC
(Directors Guild of Canada)
Canada

FIAIP
(Federazione Italiana Agenti
Immobiliari Professionali)
Italy

American Cancer Society
USA

American Diabetes Association
USA

American Hotel & Motel Association
USA

American Heart Association
USA

Girl Scouts of the USA
USA, 1977
Saul Bass

American Heart Association
USA
Lippincott

The Bond Market Association
USA, 1998
Chermayeff & Geismar: Steff Geissbuhler

Thames Valley Housing
United Kingdom

Cotton Incorporated
USA

Writers Guild of Canada
Canada

AAMA (American Amusement
Machine Association)
USA

IG Metall
Germany

Ekoland
Poland

ISSF (International Shooting
Sport Federation)
Germany

REALTOR

Realtor
USA

GEF (Global
Environment Facility)
USA

Chemical Industries Association
United Kingdom

PADI (Professional Association
of Diving Instructors)
USA, 1966
Ralph Erickson

Retail Motor Industry Federation
United Kingdom

IATSE (International Alliance of
Theatrical Stage Employees)
USA/Canada

IAFF (International Association
of Fire Fighters)
USA

IPSSA (Independent
Pool and Spa ssociation)
USA

Food and Agriculture
Organization (FAO)
Italy

World Federation of the
Sporting Goods Industry
Switzerland, ca 1978

Banner of Peace
USA, 1931
Nicholas Roerich

NFPA International
USA

Scouts Canada
Canada

YMCA (Young Men's
Christian Association)
USA, 2003

Better Business Bureau
(BBB)
USA/Canada

 association for the advancement of baltic studies

AABS
USA

IATA (International Air
Transport Association)
Canada

ABAV (Associação Brasileira
de Agências de Viagens)
Brazil

Boys & Girls Clubs of America (BGCA)
USA, 1980

Prevent Child Abuse America
USA

Slow Food
Italy

Independent Pictures
Switzerland

AAA
Australia

NSA (National
Speakers Association)
USA

Rotary International
USA, 1923

Type Directors Club (TDC)
USA, 1994
Gerard Huerta

MEF (Maskinentrepreneurenes Forbund)
Norway

DISK
Turkey

**AAL (Aid Association
for Lutherans)**
USA

Plus
USA, 2005
Pentagram

**CYO (The Catholic
Youth Organization)**
USA

Civitan International
USA

Sports Car Club of America
USA

Automobile Club of Southern California
USA

Columbiettes
USA

CORSA (Corvair Society of America)
USA

Family Motor
Coach Association
USA

Motion Picture Association
of America Inc (MPAA)
USA

DSA (Direct Selling Association)
USA

Svit (Swiss Real Estate Association)
Switzerland

NVF
Netherlands, 2003
SoDesign

VDE
Germany

ABA (American Bar Association)
USA

Gama
USA

**NAHI (National Association
of Home Inspectors)**
USA

**AFDEC (Association of Franchised
Distributors of Electronic Components)**
United Kingdom

VNG (Vereniging van
Nederlandse Gemeenten)
Netherlands

DFCG (Association Nationale des Directeurs
Financiers et de Contrôle de Gestion)
France

AARP (formerly American
Association of Retired Persons)
USA, 2007

UKWA
United Kingdom, 2009

Filmplus, Forum für Filmschnitt und Montagekunst
(Forum for film editing)
Germany

ADMA (Aviation Distributors and
Manufacturers Association)
USA

DIF (Sistema Nacional para el
Desarrollo Integral de la Familia)
Mexico

SIA (Securities Industry
Association)
United Kingdom

Democratic Party
USA

Grand Old Party (GOP)
USA

SDP (Socijaldemokratska Partija Hrvatske/
Social Democratic Party of Croatia)
Croatia

HSLS (Hrvatska socijalno liberalna stranka/
Croatian Social Liberal Party)
Croatia, ca 1999

Barack Obama Presidential Campaign
USA, 2007
Sender

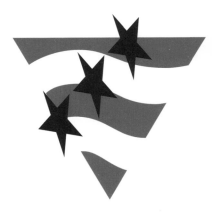

National Stonewall Democrats
USA

Republican National Convention
USA, 2008

Conservative Party
United Kingdom, 2006
Perfect Day

Labour Party
United Kingdom

Solidarnosc
Poland, 1980
Jerzy Janiszewski

**PSL (Polskie Stronnictwo Ludowe/
Polish People's Party)**
Poland

Parti Socialiste/Socialist Party
France

242

RAF (Red Army Faction)
Germany

Folkpartiet liberalerna/
Liberal People's Party
Sweden

Partido Socialista/Socialist Party
Portugal

ALF (Animal Liberation Front)
United Kingdom

SP. (Socialistische
Partij/Socialist Party)
Netherlands, 2006
Thonik

CDU

CDU (Christlich
Demokratische Union
Deutschlands)
Germany, 2003

FDIC (Federal Deposit
Insurance Corporation)
USA, 1974

Grand Old Party (GOP)
USA

SHCP (Secretaria de
Hacienda y Credito Publico)
Mexico

ICC Berlin
(Internationale Congress Centrum Berlin)
Germany

INC (Instituto Nacional de Cultura)
Peru

MotorCities
USA

World Customs Organization (WCO)
Belgium, 1993

Hong Kong Sports Development Board
China

ros.gov.uk

ros.gov.uk
United Kingdom, 2009
RR Donnelley

IMSS (Instituto Mexicano
del Segura Social)
Mexico, 1992

DEUTSCHE MESSE AG

Deutsche Messe AG
Germany, 1947
Paul Rademacher

Government of
Saskatchewan
Canada

Maryland-National
Capital Park and
Planning Commission
USA

GSA
USA

Dallas
USA

Foodland Ontario
Canada
The Watt Group

SNAP (Supplemental Nutrition
Assistance Program)
USA

U.S. Air Force
USA, 2000
Siegel+Gale

Finnish Road Administration
Finland

GMPTE (Transport for
Greater Manchester)
United Kingdom

Equal Housing
Opportunity
USA, 1988

FEHB (Federal Employees
Health Benefits)
USA

Department of Health
& Human Services
USA

American Revolution Bicentennial
USA, 1975
Chermayeff & Geismar: Bruce Blackburn

Department of Energy
USA, 1977

Department
of Commerce
USA, 1913

Department of Justice
Office of Justice
Programs
USA

DHCC (Deployment
Health Clinical Center)
USA, ca 2001

Peace Corps
USA, 1961

Senior Corps
USA

The White House
USA

CIA
(Central Intelligence Agency)
USA, 1950

NASA (National Aeronautics
and Space Administration)
USA, 1976
Danne & Blackburn

248

Civil Defense
USA, 1939
N. W. Ayer: Charles T. Coiner

Civil Defense
Switzerland

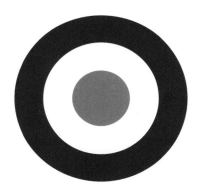

Royal Air Force
United Kingdom, 1947

NATO
Belgium

**NASA (National Aeronautics
and Space Administration)**
USA, 1959
James Modarelli

Bundeswehr
Germany

82nd Airborne Division
USA, 1917

United States Coast Guard
USA, 1968
Raymond Loewy

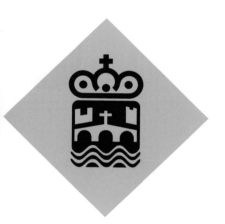

Deputación de Pontevedra
Spain

Deniz Yollari
Turkey

Département du
Val de Marne
France

OSCE (Organization for Security
and Co-operation in Europe)
Austria

EADS (European Aeronautic
Defence and Space Command)
Netherlands, 2000

SMM
Germany

ESA
(European Space Agency)
France

National Lottery
Commission
United Kingdom

Pôle emploi
France, ca 2008

National Park Service
USA, 1951/2001

Greenland Home Rule
Greenland, 2004
Bysted

I Love New York More Than Ever
USA, 2001
Milton Glaser

I Love New York
USA, 1977
Milton Glaser

FDA
(Food & Frug Administration)
USA

NYC (New York City)
USA, 2007
Wolff Olins

Le Cube
France

America Supports You
USA, 2004

Visit Britain
United Kingdom

Morocco
Morocco

Visit Denmark
Denmark

Definitely Dubai
Dubai

South Africa, It's Possible
South Africa

Brasil
Brazil, 2005
Kiko Farkas

Argentina
Argentina, 2006
Guillermo Brea & Associates:
Alejandro Luna, Carolina Mikalef

Japan
Japan

España
Spain, 1983
Joan Miró

Croatia
Croatia

Ireland
Ireland

Malta
Malta

France
France, 2009

254

City of Melbourne
Australia, 2009
Landor Associates

Quito
Ecuador, 2009

 Gemeente Breda

Gemeente Breda
Netherlands

 Jernbaneverket

Jernbanaverket
Norway

Finland
Finland

Greece
Greece

Maldives
Maldives, 2011
Quo Keen

Switzerland
Switzerland

Scotland
United Kingdom

Slovakia
Slovakia

México
Mexico

The Land Registry
United Kingdom, 2003
North

Aicep Portugal Global
Portugal

Vivir Mejor
Mexico, 2008

National Park Service
USA, 1966
Chermayeff & Geismar

Taiwan – The Heart of Asia
Taiwan, 2011
Winkreative

United States Postal Service
USA, 1993

Post Danmark
Denmark, 1993
Studio Dumbar, Kontrapunkt

DPD
(Deutscher Paket Dienst)
Germany

Posten
Sweden

La Poste/De Post Group
Belgium, 2008
Sign*

PTT Post
Netherlands

Correos
Spain

TNT
Netherlands, 1998
KSDP

FedEx
USA, 1994
Landor Associates: Lindon Leader

Hellenic Post (Elta)
Greece

Post Office
United Kingdom

UPS
USA, 2003
FutureBrand

Go! Express & Logistics
Germany

Russian Post
Russia

Federal Express
USA, 1974
Richard Runyon

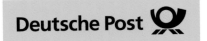

Deutsche Post
Germany, 1998
Nitsch Design

La Poste
France

Canada Post
Canada

DHL
Germany, 2003
Nitsch Design

U.S. Mail
USA, 1970
Raymond Loewy

CTT Correios
Portugal, 2004
Brandia Central

Royal Mail
United Kingdom, 1990

Correos Chile
Chile, 2008
Grupo Oxigeno

University of Cambridge
United Kingdom

University of Oxford
United Kingdom

The City
University
of
New York

City University of New York
USA, 2008
Pentagram

Kid
Knowledge

Kid Knowledge
USA, 2009
Danne Design

UniSA

UniSA
(University of South Australia)
Australia

NIIGATA
INSTITUTE OF
TECHNOLOGY

Niigita Institute of Technology
Japan

UCSF (University of
California San Francisco)
USA, 2007

NAIT (The Northern Aberta
Institute of Technology)
Canada

codarts

hogeschool voor de kunsten

Codarts
Netherlands, 2005
75B

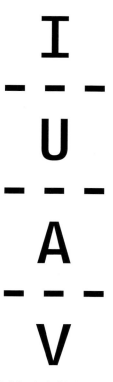

Pont-Aven School of Contemporary Art
USA, 2008
Pentagram

MIT
(Massachusetts Institute of Technology)
USA, 2003
Tim Blackburn, Matthew Carter

Yale

Yale University
USA

Education First
United Kingdom

SAIC (School of the Art
Institute of Chicago)
USA

IUAV (Istituto Universitario di Architettura di Venezia)
Italy, 2002
Phillipe Apeloig

PPSEC Accredited
Canada

The Ivy League
USA

The Open University
United Kingdom

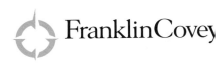

FranklinCovey
USA

Learning Tree International
USA

Glendale Community College
USA

Florida Gulf Coast University
USA

National Academy
for Nuclear Training
USA

The Cooper Union
USA, 2009
Doyle Partners

DeVry University
USA

**AAAA (Arte, Arquitectura,
Antropología y Autoritarismo)**
Venezuela, 2007
Santiago Pol

Columbia Business School
USA, 2007
Pentagram: Michael Bierut

**UPC
(BarcelonaTech)**
Spain

TU Wien
Austria

Yale
USA

Malmö Högskola
Sweden, 1998

V&A
United Kingdom, 1989
Alan Fletcher

Musée d'Orsay
France

Guggenheim
USA, 2009
Pentagram: Abbott Miller, John Kudos

9/11
MEMORIAL

9/11 Memorial
USA, 2009
Landor Associates

MoMA

MoMa
(Museum of Modern Art)
USA

BALTIC

Baltic
United Kingdom, 1998
Henrik Nygren Design, Greger Ulf Nilson

SFMOMA (San Francisco
Museum of Modern Art)
USA

ICA

ICA (Institute of
Contemporary Arts)
United Kingdom

CCEBA
Argentina, 2004
Bernardo+Celis

Kingsway Exhibitions
United Kingdom

Whatcom Museum
USA

Imperial War Museum
United Kingdom
Minale Tattersfield: Paul Astbury

MUSEE OLYMPIQUE
LAUSANNE

Musée Olympique
(Olympic Museum)
Switzerland

Design Exchange (DX)
Canada

Tate
United Kingdom, 1999
Wolff Olins

Museo de Palpa
Peru, 2003
Ideo Comunicadores

Museu Ciência e Vida
Brazil, 2009
Tecnopop

iF
Germany

Museon
Netherlands, 2003
Faydherbe & De Vringer

Science Museum
United Kingdom, 2010
*johnson banks: Michael Johnson,
Kath Tudball, Miho Aishima*

Museum of the Moving Image
USA, 2011
karlssonwilker

Museum of Chinese in America
USA, 2011
Pentagram: Michael Bierut, Yve Ludwig

Maac
(Museo Antropologico y de
Arte Contemporaneo)
Ecuador, 2000
Versus: Peter Mussfeldt

John F. Kennedy Presidential
Library and Museum
USA, 1964
Chermayeff & Geismar

American Folk Art Museum
USA, 2000
Pentagram

NGA
(National Gallery of Australia)
Australia

**DEUTSCHE
KINEMATHEK
MUSEUM
FÜR FILM UND
FERNSEHEN**

Museum für Film und Fernsehen
Germany, 2006
Pentagram

CALIFORNIA
ACADEMY OF
SCIENCES

California Academy of Sciences
USA, 2007
Pentagram

Museum of Sex
USA
Pentagram

GAGOSIAN GALLERY

Gagosian Gallery
USA

Design Museum
United Kingdom, 2003
Graphic Thought Facility

PRINCETON
UNIVERSITY
ART MUSEUM

Princeton University Art Museum
USA, 2005
Pentagram

Museo del Niño
Ecuador, 2009
Latinbrand

Good Design Award
Japan

National Gallery of Art
USA

Rock and Roll
Hall of Fame and Museum
USA

RMN (Réunion des Muséses Nationaux)
France

Detroit Institute of Arts
USA, 2008
Pentagram

270

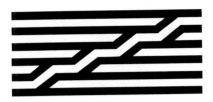

Centre Pompidou
France, 1977
Visual Design Association: Jean Widmer

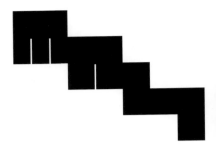

Mali
(Museo de Arte de Lima)
Peru, 2004
Studioa

Orlando Museum of Art (OMA)
USA, 2008
Push

Museum of Arts and Design
USA, 2008
Pentagram

Gas As Interface
Japan

Insight
Brazil

Mills
USA

Red Dot Design Award
Germany

Design Museum
United Kingdom

Luxo ASA
Norway

Buongiorno
Italy

National Maritime Museum
(Darling Harbour)
Australia

National Baseball Hall
of Fame and Museum
USA

272

DQS (Deutsche Gesellschaft zur
Zertifizierung von Managementsystemen)
Germany

Kodak Colorwatch system
USA

USB
(Universal Serial Bus)
USA

DTS
USA, 2007

3M MCS Warranty
USA

Biohazard
USA, 1966

Radura
Netherlands, 1960s

Der Grüne Punkt
Germany

C-Tick
Australia

i.Link
Japan

Conforms to BS5665
United Kingdom

**Radioactive
(Hazard symbol)**
USA

Recycling Symbol
USA, 1970
Gary Anderson

Papier recyclé
France

Woolmark
Australia, 1964
Francesco Saroglia

Australian Made
Australia, 1986
Ken Cato

Dolphin Safe
USA, 1990

Farm Quality Assured
Northern Ireland
United Kingdom

U.S. Grade A
USA

Hecho en México
(Made in Mexico)
Mexico

Ceylon Tea
Sri Lanka

Made in America
USA

Made in USA Brand
USA

Dekra
Germany

BuiltGreen
Canada

Canada Tsuga
Japan/Canada

Type Tested
Australia

Glass Recycles
USA

Varefakta Kontrolleret
Sweden, 2011

Energy Star
USA

Tax Free Shopping
European Union

Varefakta Kontrolleret
Sweden

Crime
Let's Bring It Down
United Kingdom

Rainforest Alliance Certified
USA

Recycle
United Kingdom
Gardiner Richardson

ISO
(International Organization for Standardization)
Switzerland

Fairtrade
Germany

Real California Cheese
USA

Schwinn
(quality seal)
USA

DTS Digital Surround
USA, 1991

TSE
(Turkish Standard Institution)
Turkey

DVD
Japan, 1990s

DV
(Digital Video)
Japan, 1994

GSM
United Kingdom

HDCD
(High Definition Compatible Digital)
USA

Rx
USA

CE
(Conformité Européenne)
European Union, 1993

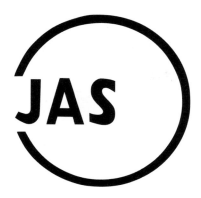

JAS
(Japanese Agricultural Standards)
Japan

CSA
(Canadian Standards Association)
Canada

JAS
(Japanese Agricultural Standards)
Japan

UL Classification mark
USA/Canada, ca 1903

Kitemark
United Kingdom, 1903

Registered Trademark
USA

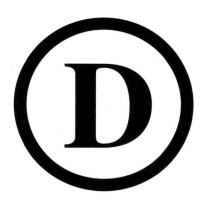

Demko
Denmark

PG
(Parental Guidance Suggested
MPAA Movie Rating)
USA

Restricted
MPAA Movie Rating
USA

Parental Advisory
Explicit Content
USA, ca 2000

Adults Only (AO)
ESRB Rating
USA, 1994

Dolby Surround
USA

Dolby
USA, 2008
Turner Duckworth

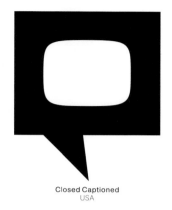

Closed Captioned
USA

Closed Captioned
USA, ca 1972
WGBH-TV: Jack Foley

DAB
(Digital Audio Broadcasting)
Netherlands

Direct Stream Digital
(DSD)
Japan/Netherlands

LaserDisc
USA, 1981

Digital Data Storage
(DDS)
Japan

RDS (Radio Data System)
United Kingdom/USA
BBC

USTA
USA, 2006
USTA, Siegel+Gale

WTA
(Women's Tennis Association)
USA

FFT
(Fédération Française de Tennis)
France

Tennis Australia
Australia

FFBB
(Fédération Française de Basketball)
France, 2010
Graphèmes

Dubai Sports Council
United Arab Emirates, ca 2005

FIFA
(Fédération Internationale de Football Association)
Switzerland

FiA
(Fédération Internationale de l'Automobile)
France

**Real Madrid Club
de Fútbol**
Spain, 2001

Russian Football Union
Russia

**IRFU (Irish Rugby
Football Union)**
Ireland

KNVB
Netherlands
SoDesign

DVTK 1910
Hungary

Arsenal Football Club
United Kingdom, 2002

Boca Juniors
Argentina, 2007
Diseño Shakespear

Futbol Club Barcelona
Spain

FC Dietikon
Switzerland

MKE Ankaragücü
Turkey

Chicago Cubs
USA

Borussia Dortmund
Germany
SoDesign

284

Chelsea Football Club
United Kingdom

Norges Ischockeyforbund
Norway

Colorado State Rams
USA

Pumas de la UNAM
Mexico

F.C. København
Denmark

**Danmarks
Ishockey Union**
Denmark

**FFS
(Fédération Française de Ski)**
France

Little League Baseball
USA

Toronto Blue Jays
Canada, 2004

Ajax Amsterdam
Netherlands, 1990
Samenwerkende Ontwerpers: Andre Toet

Paris Saint-Germain
Football Club
France

Serie A TIM
Italy, 2009

Detroit Pistons
USA

Indiana Fever
USA, 2000

FC Bayern München
Germany
SoDesign

Celtic Football Club
United Kingdom, ca 1995

Hamilton Tiger-Cats
Canada

Durham Bulls
USA, 1998

FC Steaua Bucuresti
Romania, 2003

Dynamo Kyiv
Ukraine

AC Verona
Italy

Colorado Mammoth
USA, 2001

FC Dallas
USA, 2005

Unión de Rugby del Uruguay
Uruguay

Los Angeles Lakers
USA, 2011

Olympique de Marseille
France

Los Angeles Dodgers
(cap logo)
USA, 1958

New York Yankees
(cap logo)
USA

CFL
Canada, 1970

NFL (National Football
League)
USA, 2008

New York Yankees
USA, 1970s

Premier League
United Kingdom

Columbus Clippers
USA

Redskins
USA, 1970

Army Black Knights
USA, 1994

Marshall Thundering Herd
USA

Iowa Hawkeyes
USA, 1979

Detroit Red Wings
USA, ca 1982

Appalachian League
USA

Chicago Bulls
USA, 1966
Dean P. Wessel

Cleveland Indians
USA, 1980

Louisville Cardinals
USA

Fußball-Bundesliga
Germany

LFP
(Ligue de Football Professionnel)
France

RFU England Rugby
United Kingdom

NBA
(National Basketball Association)
USA, 1969
Siegel+Gale

U.S. Figure Skating
USA, 2003

The Football League
United Kingdom, 2004

Olympic symbol
Switzerland, 1913
Pierre de Coubertin

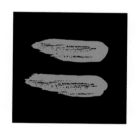

WORLD ANTI-DOPING AGENCY

play true

WADA
(World Anti-Doping Agency)
Canada

NASCAR
(National Association for
Stock Car Auto Racing)
USA

IRB
(International
Rugby Board)
Ireland

WSL
(World Surf League)
USA

INDUSTRY

AEROSPACIAL
AGRICULTURAL
AIRPLANE MANUFACTURERS
& SERVICING
AUTOMOBILE, SERVICING
& SUPPLIES
CHEMICAL INDUSTRIES
ELECTRONICS
ENGINEERING COMPANIES
INDUSTRIAL CONGLOMERATES
MARINE INDUSTRY
MOBILITY
MOTORBIKES
OPTICAL COMPANIES
STEEL & MINING

Mini
United Kingdom, 2001
Interbrand Zintzmeyer & Lux

Bentley
United Kingdom

Aston Martin
United Kingdom, 1987

Chrysler
USA, 2007
SVP Design: Trevor Creed

Moto Guzzi
Italy

Ducati
Italy, 1967

Citroën
France, 2009
Landor Associates

Peugeot
France, 2010
BETC Design

Opel
Germany, 1987

Saturn
USA, 1987

Peugeot
France, 1998

Holden
Australia, 1994

Citroën
France, 1985

Mitsubishi
Japan

Toyota
Japan

Audi
Germany, 1994
Sedley Place

Nissan
Japan, 1984

Fiat
Italy, 2011
Robilant Associati

Lancia
Italy, 2007
Robilant Associati

Ducati
Italy, 2008

Nissan
Japan, 2000
FutureBrand

Dacia
Germany

Rolls-Royce
United Kingdom
Tatham Pearce

Firestone
USA

Freightliner Trucks
USA

Fenco Truck Accessories
USA

Edelbrock
USA

Öhlins
Sweden

Brembo
Italy

Castrol Motor Oil
United Kingdom, 2006

MG
United Kingdom, 1924

General Motors (GM)
USA

Delco Electronics
USA

Delco Systems
USA

ACDelco
USA

Fel-Pro
USA

Norton Triumph
United Kingdom, 1970s

GMC Truck
USA

Ford Trucks
USA, 2001

Peterson
USA

AAMCO Transmissions
USA

AD
Belgium

American Motors
USA, 1970

298

Ford
USA
The Partners

Land Rover
United Kingdom, 1986
Tatham Pearce: David Pearce

Kia Motors
South Korea

STP
USA
Armored AutoGroup Inc

Hella
Germany

Yamalube
USA

Magneti Marelli
Italy

Smart
Germany

Riken
France

FAG
Germany

DAF
Netherlands

Falken
USA

ACDelco
USA

BFGoodrich Tires
USA

Denso
Japan

Isuzu
Japan

Ryco Filters
Australia

DeLorean Motor Company
(DMC)
USA

TomTom
Netherlands, 2007
TBWA\Neboko: Matthew Harvey

Ducati
Italy, 1987

Navistar
USA

Polaris
USA

Coastal
USA

Allison Transmission
USA

Filtri Tecnocar
Italy

Federal-Mogul
USA

Road Demon
USA

FP Diesel
USA

Goodyear
USA, 1900

Rexton
South Korea

Triumph Motorcycles
United Kingdom, 2005

Fox Racing Shox
USA

Rain-X
Netherlands

Ducati
Italy

America's Tire Co.
USA

Discount Tire Co. Inc.
USA

Honda Powersports
Japan

Honda Powersports
Japan
Miles Newlyn

Mallard
USA

Jayco
USA

Hankook
South Korea

Purolator
Canada

Maruti Suzuki
India, 2011

Ssang Yong
South Korea

Ashok Leyland
India

Safety-Kleen
USA

Weber
Italy

Valvoline
USA

Kent
United Kingdom

Lada
Russia

Kitaco
Japan

Leer
USA

PIAGGIO

Piaggio
Italy

Jeep
USA

GReddy
Japan

NAVISTAR ™

Navistar
USA

PACCAR Inc

Paccar Inc
USA

COBRA

Cobra
USA

IVECO

Iveco
Italy

BULAVTO

Bulauto
Bulgaria

HUMMER

Hummer
USA, 1992

bosal

Bosal
Belgium

momo

Momo
Italy

MAHLE

Mahle
Germany

Michelin
France

Fiat
Italy, 1967
Jean Reiwald, Armin Vogt

Pirelli
Italy, 1945

Speedy
Canada

Smart
Germany, 1994

Quick Brake
Denmark

Lincoln Electric
USA

Continental
Germany

BRIDGESTONE

Bridgestone
Japan, 2011

Firestone

Firestone
USA

Jeep

Jeep
USA

FRAM
Filters

Fram Filters
USA

GMC

GMC
USA

RAC

RAC
United Kingdom, 1997
North

KTM
Austria

NGK

NGK
Japan

TRICO

Trico
USA

Prestone

Prestone
USA

California Side Car Inc
USA

Braggin Waggon
USA

Courtesy Transportation
USA

Courtesy Transportation
USA

Com4Wheels
Germany

The Pickup Guy
USA

Betten
USA

D B Wilson
United Kingdom

Ford Motor Company

Ford Motor Company
USA

Raybestos
USA, 1900s

Norton
United Kingdom, 1913
James Lansdowne Norton

Daewoo Matiz
South Korea

Vespa
Italy

Landini
Canada

Lambretta
Italy

Pininfarina
Italy

Jaguar
United Kingdom, 2002
The Partners: Greg Quinton, Steve Owen, Helen Cooley

Deflecta-Shield
USA

DeLorean
USA

Alvis
United Kingdom

Harley-Davidson
USA, 1965

310

Tesla
USA

Ferrari
Italy, 1947

Maserati
Italy, 1914
Mario Maserati

Rover
United Kingdom

Champion
USA

Dellorto
Italy

Seat
Spain
Enterprise IG

Suzuki
Japan

Daewoo
South Korea

Daihatsu
Japan

Hankook
South Korea

Dunlop Tyres
United Kingdom

Marchal
France

Tein
Japan

Kawasaki
Japan

Sachs
Germany

312

Pep Boys Auto
USA

Lita
France, 1965

Tatra
Czech Republic

Victory Motorcycles
USA, 1997

Cooper Tires
USA, 1950s

Alpine
France

Mack Trucks
USA, 1921

Peterbilt
USA

Bugatti
France

BMW
Germany, 1979
Franz Josef Popp

VW
Germany, 2000
MetaDesign

Saab
Sweden, 2000

Vauxhall
United Kingdom, 2009

Maybach
Germany

AGV
Italy

Dunlop Tyres
United Kingdom, 1962
Design Research Unit

Chrysler
USA, 1962
*Lippincott & Margulies:
Robert Stanley*

Corvette
USA, 1953
Robert Bartholomew

Air Lift
USA, 1949

Rieger
Germany

BorgWarner
USA

Corvette
USA

Pontiac
USA, 2006

Mercedes-Benz
Germany, 1988
Kurt Weidemann

Infiniti
Japan, 2004
Lippincott Mercer

Lincoln
USA

Lexus
Japan, 2002
Siegel+Gale

Acura
Japan, 1991

Honda Automobiles
Japan
Miles Newlyn

Hyundai
South Korea

Man
Germany

Chevrolet
USA, 2004

Audi
Germany, 2009
Rayan Abdullah

Lamborghini
Italy

Lotus
United Kingdom, 1952

Proton
Malaysia

Saab-Scania
Sweden, 1984
Carl Frederik Reuterswärd

Skoda
Czech Republic, 2011

Chevrolet Impala
USA

Volvo
Sweden

Opel
Germany, 2002

DAIMLER

Daimler
Germany, 2007
Schindler Parent Identity, Underware

DAIMLERCHRYSLER

DaimlerChrysler
Germany, 1998

Porsche
Germany

Alfa Romeo
Italy, 1992
Robilant Associati

Cadillac
USA, 1999
Anne-Marie LaVerge-Webb

ZENETTI

Zenetti Wheels
Australia

Subaru
Japan

Renault
France, 2007

Buick
USA, 2002

Subaru/Fuji Heavy
Industries
Japan, 1953

Oldsmobile
USA, 1981

Mazda
Japan, 1997
Rei Yoshimara

Dodge
USA, 1993

Oldsmobile
USA

Buick
USA, 1990s

Airbus
France, 2010

Boeing
USA, 1997
Rick Eiber

Agusta Westland
Italy/United Kingdom, ca 2000

Fokker
Netherlands

Goodrich
USA, 2001
Kass Uehling

Rockwell Collins
USA, 2006
BrandLogic: Randell Holder,
Fredy Jaggi, Gene Grossman

Learjet

Learjet
Canada

BOMBARDIER

Bombardier
Canada

DIEHL

Diehl
Germany

Stork
Netherlands

Cessna

Cessna
USA

Aena

Aena
(Aeropuertos Españoles y Navegación Aérea)
Spain

McDonnell Douglas
USA, 1967

EMBRAER

Embraer
Brazil

FalconJet

FalconJet
France

Messerschmitt
Germany

NAA (North American
Aviation)
USA

International Airlines Group (IAG)
United Kingdom/Spain, 2011
Bostock & Pollitt

IAI
(Israel Aerospace Industries)
Israel

Dryden Flight Research Center
USA, 1998

Enkes
Netherlands

United Space Alliance
USA, 1990s

Boston Whaler
USA

DUNCAN
AVIATION

Mako Marine
USA

Duncan Aviation
USA, 1989
Mitchell Mauk

ENAV
Italy

Plastimo
France

Newport Boats
USA

Piper Aircraft
USA

Elliott Aviation
USA

J/Boats
USA

Wellcraft
USA

Harken
USA

Laser
Australia

Mariner
United Kingdom

North Sails
USA

Scubapro
USA

Chaparral Boats
USA

Nanni Diesel
Italy

Chris-Craft Boats
USA

Technisub
Italy

Four Winns
USA

Hobie
USA

Tartan Yachts
USA

Evinrude
USA

Scarab
USA

Zeppelin
France

Hägglunds Drives
Sweden

326

V33 Group
France

3M
USA, 1977
Siegel+Gale

USX
USA, 1991

IHI
Japan

WEG
Brazil

George Fischer
Switzerland

Dayco
USA

ABS
Sweden

NOK
Japan

Olin
USA

Cintas
USA

Eaton
Italy

Schindler

Schindler
Switzerland, 2006

HELGELAND
HOLDING

Helgeland Holding
Norway

International Environmental
USA

BlueScope Steel
Australia

AALBORG WHITE

Aalborg White
Denmark

Wienerberger
Austria

Ferrous
Brazil, 2007
Hardy Design: Mariana Hardy

Macmahon
Australia

ICA
(Industria Chimica Adriatica)
Italy

Amoco
USA. 1970

Westfalia
Germany

Pall
USA

Werner
USA

SCA (Svenska Cellulosa
Aktiebolaget)
Sweden. 1990
Pentagram

SEM
USA

Glidden Paint
USA

Gates Corporation
USA

Duni
Sweden

Krylon
USA

Weiss Technik
Germany

Zeiss
Germany, 1993

Atlas Copco
Sweden

NIBCO
USA

Vassallo
Puerto Rico

DAF
Turkey

Ajax
USA

UNION CARBIDE

Union Carbide
USA

BORDEN

Borden Foods
USA

Toro
USA

LTR Germany
Germany

Panametrics
USA

Plannja
Sweden

Air Products
USA

Dust-Off
Canada

DSME (Daewoo Shipbuilding
& Marine Engineering)
South Korea

Gardner Denver
USA

Grainger
USA

Colt Industries

Colt Industries
USA

KAWASAKI STEEL

Kawasaki Steel
Japan

ArcelorMittal
Luxembourg

Severstal
Russia

Ahlstrom
Finland, 2001
Porkka & Kuutsa

Papyrus
Sweden

Johnson Controls
USA, 2007
Lippincott

Essar Steel
India

De Dietrich

De Dietrich
France

Glunz & Jensen
Denmark

Mistral Paints
Czech Republic

Usiminas
Brazil

Glynwed Pipe Systems
United Kingdom

Alcan Cable
USA

Dustbane
Canada

Fireseal
Sweden

Rock Oil
United Kingdom

Canson
France

WideLite

Wide-Lite
USA

Port-O-Let

Port-O-Let
USA

valspar

Valspar
USA, 2011

sappi

Sappi
South Africa

De Beers

De Beers
South Africa, 2002
The Partners: Michael Paisley, Rob Holloway

**Rockwell
Automation**

Rockwell Automation
USA, 2001

Linde
Germany, 2004
Peter Schmidt Group

Westside Concrete Materials
USA

Republicsteel

Rebublic Steel
USA

wausauPAPER

Wausau Paper
USA, 2004

TREBRUK

Trebruk
Sweden

LESJÖFORS

Lesjöfors
Sweden

International Paper Company
USA, 1961
Lester Beall Associates

Dalum Papir
Denmark

Paper Products Design
Germany

HOYA

Hoya
Japan

Coral

Coral (Tintas Coral)
Brazil

Holley

Holley
USA

Dulux

Dulux
United Kingdom

NUCOR

Nucor
USA

Tektronix

Tektronix
USA

LKAB

LKAB
(Luossavaara-Kiirunavaara Aktiebolag)
Sweden

SSAB

SSAB
Sweden

WATTYL

Wattyl
Australia

TEIJIN

Teijin Limited
Japan

LIEBHERR

Liebherr Group
Switzerland

ANDRiTZ

Andritz
Austria

ANIXTER

Anixter
USA

rotork

Rotork
United Kingdom

KlauKe

Klauke
Germany

VOITH

Voith
Germany

INCO

Inco
Canada

SOKKIA

Sokkia
Japan

POSCO

Posco
South Korea

Teksid
Italy

CompAir
United Kingdom

Gunnebo Fastening
Sweden

Superior Essex
USA

Jason Industrial Inc
USA

Fairchild
USA

Norske Skog
Norway

International Paint
United Kingdom

Rhodia
France

IR Bobcat
USA

Geberit
USA

Curragh
Australia

SGL Carbon Group
Germany

Crown Cork & Seal
USA

Steel Dynamics Inc
USA

Furukawa
Brazil

BührmannUbbens
Netherlands, 2004
TelDesign

Weyerhaeuser
USA

Mondi
South Africa

Mapei
Italy

Weil-McLain
USA

Kennametal
USA

China Steel
China

Tohatsu
Japan

Airwell
France

Yokohama
Japan

Vicson
Venezuela

Pemsa Cable Management Systems
Spain

Weiler
USA

Wega
Italy, 1980s

Georgia-Pacific

Georgia-Pacific
USA

Tetra Pak

Tetra Pak
Switzerland, 1992
Toni Manhart, Jörgen Haglind

vallourec

Vallourec
France

outokumpu

Outokumpu
Finland

 **JAEGER**

Jaeger
Germany

Triton

Triton
USA

 **NKK**

NKK Group
Japan

BHP

BHP
Australia

 **HUBER GRUPPE**

Huber Gruppe
Germany

 **LEROY SOMER**

Leroy-Somer
France

LPS
USA, ca 1961

Rebasa
Mexico

Nalco
USA

Plâtres Lambert
Belgium

Tosoh
Japan

ACO
Canada

Putzmeister
Germany

Ebara
Japan

Nippon Paint
Japan

British Steel
United Kingdom

Oloid
Switzerland

Boise Cascade Corporation
USA, 2002
Siegel+Gale

Vermeer
USA

Tecumseh
USA

Bobcat
USA, ca 2007

Whale
United Kingdom

Crenlo
USA

Nerco
USA

AK Steel
USA

Alesco
Japan

Alcoa
USA, 1999
Arnold Saks Associates

Tata Steel
India, 1999
Wolff Olins

Aracruz
Brazil

Noranda
Canada

Champion International
USA

Abitibi Consolidated
Canada

African Gold
United Kingdom

Moldavkabel
Moldavia

Sealed Air
USA

Facet
USA

Allegheny
Technologies
USA

Villares
Brazil, 1967
Cauduro Martino

Steelmark
USA, 1960

GE
USA, 2004
Wolff Olins

Klabin
Brazil, 1979
Alexandre Wollner

Deft
USA

Monsanto
USA

**Package Steel Building
Systems**
USA

**CAMPSA (Compañía Arrendataria
del Monopolio del Petróleo)**
Spain

Tokyo Steel
Japan

Omaha Paper
USA

P&L (Pratt & Lambert)
USA

USS (U.S. Steel)
USA

AkzoNobel
Netherlands, 2008
Saffron Brand Consultants, Martin Rijven, Pentagram

Caparol
Germany, 1984
Luigi Colani

Olympic Paints & Stains
USA

Yoppi
Hungary

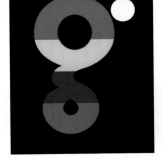

General Paint
Canada

Gentry Living Color
USA, 1993
Paul Rand

PYE
United Kingdom

Philips
Netherlands, 1995

Pramac
Italy

Rexel
France

Ingram Micro
USA

Gold Peak Group
China

Tact Precision
Taiwan

Tecatel
Spain

FERMAX

Fermax
Spain

Farnell Electronics
United Kingdom

MITSUMI

Mitsumi
Japan

TERADYNE

Teradyne
USA

vidikron

Vidikron
USA

xantrex

Xantrex
USA

GENELEC

Genelec
Finland

ALESIS

Alesis
USA

AEG

AEG
Germany, 2000

TEAC

TEAC
Japan

Murata
USA, ca 1947

QSC Audio
USA, 2002

TOSHIBA

Toshiba
Japan

RICOH

Ricoh
Japan

Quasar
USA

UHER

Uher
Germany

ALLIED

Allied
USA

Oppo
Netherlands, 2004
Studio Dumbar

NEC

NEC
Japan, 1992
Landor Associates

Sanyo
Japan, 1987

348

Daewoo Electronics
South Korea

FLEXTRONICS X

Flextronics
Singapore

Tyco Electronics
Switzerland/USA

Tyco Electronics

Tyco Electronics
Switzerland/USA, 2007
Interbrand: Daniel Sim, Curt Munger

Sennheiser
Germany

beyerdynamic)))))

Beyerdynamic
Germany

Legrand
France

KYOCERA

Kyocera
Japan, 1982
Mitsuo Hosokawa

Terasaki
Japan

Crown International
USA

AEG
Germany, 1908
Peter Behrens

TDK
Japan

Sanyo
Japan, 1970s

Airtronics
USA

Mercury
USA

Sansui
Japan

Solectron
USA

Yamaichi Electronics
Japan

Seiko Instruments
Japan

Romi
Brazil, 1972
Cauduro Martino

Chicago Pneumatic
USA

Victa
Australia

Warn
USA

Veryeri Makina
Turkey

Junker Group
Germany

Fuji Heavy Industries
Japan

ThyssenKrupp
Germany

**Leucadia National
Corporation**
USA

Enron
USA, 1996
Paul Rand

Foster Wheeler
Switzerland

**PCC
(Power Corporation
of Canada)**
Canada

Samsung
South Korea, 1993
Lippincott & Margulies

LG
South Korea, 2008

Hakuto
Japan

Grupo Tampico
Mexico

Areva
France

Wesfarmers
Australia

Carlisle
USA

Doosan
South Korea
Lippincott

Franke
Switzerland

Dover
USA

Unilever
United Kingdom/Netherlands, 2005
Wolff Olins: Miles Newlyn

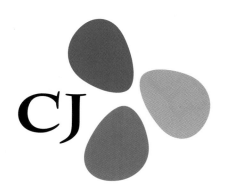

CJ
(Cheil Jedang)
South Korea

Meredith
USA, 2009
Lippincott

Kraft Foods
USA, 2009
Nitro Group, Kraft, Genesis, Landor Associates

GEA
Germany

GMR Group
India

Freudenberg
Germany

Crane
USA

354

ITT
USA, 1998
Landor Associates

Impresa
Portugal

Rockwell
USA

Votorantim
Brazil, 1999
FutureBranD

WIHURI
HANJIN

Wihuri
Finland

Hanjin
South Korea

 KANEMATSU CORPORATION

Kanematsu Corporation
Japan

Sinochem Corporation
China

United Technologies
USA

Yamaha Corporation
Japan, 1998
Rei Yoshimara

Louis Dreyfus
Netherlands

Brunswick
USA

Koch Industries
USA

Teledyne
USA, ca 2000

Lockheed Martin
USA, 1997
Anspach Grossman Enterprise: Gene Grossman

356

Time Inc.

Time Inc
USA

Time Warner

Time Warner
USA, 2003
Lippincott Mercer

vivendi

Vivendi
France, 2006
Carré Noir, Publicis

Honeywell

Honeywell
USA

VIACOM

Viacom
USA, 1990

viacom

Viacom
USA, 2006

TEXTRON

Textron
USA

ALSTOM

Alstom
France, 1998
CB'A

HITACHI

Hitachi
Japan

SIEMENS

Siemens
Germany, 1989
Mendell & Oberer

FERCO

Ferco
France

THERMAX

Thermax
India

Fletcher Building
New Zealand

Eurovia
France

 Directbouw b.v.

Directbouw
Netherlands

 e.l.m. leblanc

e.l.m leblanc
France

Travis Perkins
United Kingdom

Obayashi
Japan

Oldcastle
USA
Suzi Godson

Dufferin Concrete
Canada

CKI
China

Chubu Electric Power
Japan

Saldus Celinieks
Latvia

Depa Fysiko Aerio
Greece

Powerflush Ltd
United Kingdom

Electronorte
Brazil

Carré Bleu
France

Condor Earth
Technologies
USA

Saunier Duval
France

Meralco
Philippines

Coverd
Italy

Valley Irrigation
USA

Kogas
South Korea

VolkerWessels
Netherlands

NCC Construction
Sweden

Vinci
France, 2000s

Nevada Power Company
USA

Thermo Pride
USA

Saint-Gobain
France

Broan
USA

Wide Span Sheds
Australia

Ruud
USA

Dorma
Germany

CEMEX
Mexico

Lafarge
France

WSP Group
United Kingdom

Gentek Building Products
USA

Burnham
USA

Ariston
Italy

Dimplex
United Kingdom

Flex-a-lite
USA

Junkers
Germany

York
Canada

United Rentals
USA, 1997

Bryant Homes
United Kingdom

Redman Homes
USA

Eiffage Construction
France

Utica Boilers
USA

Gammon Skanska
China

Edison International
USA, 1996

Downer Engineering
Australia

Trane
USA

Selkirk
USA/Canada

McCulloch
USA

Allis-Chambers
USA

Sia Abrasives
Switzerland

Massey Ferguson
USA, 1958

Marathon Equipment
USA

Diamond Snow Ploughs
USA

Miller
USA

haacon
Germany

Tesco
USA

Alpego
Italy

WRIGHT TOOL

Wright Tool
USA
Sonnhalter

NEW HOLLAND

New Holland Construction
USA

Knipex
Germany

Mapal
USA

Vermont American
USA

OKUMA

Okuma
Japan

Black & Decker
USA, 2000

Craftsman
USA, 1927

Dixon
United Kingdom

ICS
USA

Wallkö
Denmark

Effer
Italy

Fassi
Italy

Bosch
Germany, 2004
United Designers Network: Erik Spiekermann

Feintool
Germany

Singer
USA

Husqvarna
Sweden, 1972

Greenlee
USA

Disston Tools
USA

DeWalt
USA

shop·vac

Shop-Vac
USA

Snap-on

Snap-on
USA

Weed Eater
USA

Komatsu
Japan

Yale Materials
USA

Genie
USA

Viking
Austria, 1980s

Wagner
Germany

Senco
USA

Ridgid
USA

Milwaukee
USA

Onan
USA

OTC
USA

Pfaff
Germany

Emco
Austria

Makita
Japan, 1991
Makita

Ko-ken
Japan

Stihl
Germany

Skil
USA

John Deere
USA, 2000

Marchesan
Brazil

Coilhose Pneumatics
USA

Ditch Witch
USA

Allied Gear
USA

Fjellman
Sweden

Kity
France

SKS Germany
Germany

Wiha Tools
Germany

Stanley
USA

Irwin Tools
USA

Facom
France

Cummins Marine
USA, 1962
Paul Rand

White Farm Equipment
USA

MEDIA, MUSIC & ENTERTAINMENT

ARTISTS & BANDS
BOOKS
CAMPAIGNS
CINEMAS & STUDIOS
DISTRIBUTORS
EVENTS & FESTIVALS
FILMS
MAGAZINES & NEWSPAPERS
MUSIC INSTRUMENTS
PUBLISHERS
RADIO
RECORD LABELS
TELEVISION CHANNELS
WEBSITES

Ghostbusters
USA, 1984
Dan Aykroyd (concept)

Jurassic Park
USA, 1993
Chip Kidd (concept)

Lucasfilm
USA

Star Wars
The Empire Strikes Back
USA, 1980

STAR WARS
RETURN OF THE JEDI

Star Wars
Return of the Jedi
USA, 1983

S.W.A.T.

S.W.A.T.
USA, 2003

SCREAM

Scream
(film)
USA, 1996

STAR WARS

Star Wars
USA, 1976
Suzy Rice

007 James Bond
USA

TRANSFORMERS

Transformers
Revenge of the Fallen
USA, 2009

The Godfather
USA, 1969
S. Neil Fujita

DreamWorks Animation
USA
Steven Spielberg, Dennis Muren, Robert Hunt

Lightstorm Entertainment
USA

Nelvana
Canada, 2004

RKO Pictures
(Radio-Keith-Orpheum)
USA

International Film Festival Rotterdam
Netherlands, 2008
75B

Amblin Entertainment
USA, 1982

Studio Ghibli
Japan

Filmax
Spain

In the City Entertainment Inc
Canada

UFA
Germany

UFA
Germany

Technicolor
USA

technicolor

Technicolor
France, 2010
Gyro:HSR, Technicolor

376

United Artists
USA, 1987

Miramax Home Entertainment
USA, 1994

Orion Home Video
USA, 1980s

NFB/ONF (National Film Board of Canada/
Office national du film du Canada)
Canada, 2002
Paprika Communications

Screen Gems
USA, 1966
Chermayeff & Geismar

Digimagen
Venezuela, 2003
Ají Pintao: Mariana Núñez

FOX

Fox
USA, 1999

IMAX

IMAX
Canada

THX
USA, ca 1983

mk2

MK2
France

P I X A R

Pixar
USA, ca 1995

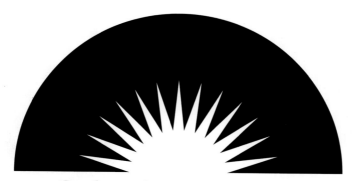

Columbia Pictures

Columbia Pictures
USA, 1976

Universal Studios
USA

Miramax Films
USA

Sony Pictures
Japan

Warner Brothers
USA

Metro-Goldwyn-Mayer
USA, 1957

Panavision
USA

Davis Entertainment
USA, 1985

Gaumont Film Company
France, ca 2004

New Line Home Entertainment
USA, 1990

Pathé
France, 1998
Landor Associates: Margaret Youngblood

Lionsgate
USA, 1997

Grease
USA, 1978

Grease 2
USA, 1982

Pathé
France

Buy 'N Large
USA, 2008

Indiana Jones
USA, 1981

Rock 'n' Roll High School
USA, 1979

Harry Potter
USA, 2001

300
USA, 1998
Frank Miller

The Warriors
USA, 1997

GRAMERCY
P I C T U R E S

Gramercy Pictures
USA

CAROLCO

Carolco
USA

Interfilm Berlin
Germany

FINE LINE
FEATURES

Fine Line Features
USA, 1991
Woody Pirtle

20th Century Fox
USA, 1935
Emil Kosa Jr

Mikros Image
France

Paramount Pictures
USA, 1974

Walt Disney Pictures
USA, 1985

Scanbox Entertainment
Denmark

United International Pictures
USA, 2001

Legendary Pictures
USA, ca 2000

Touchstone Home Entertainment
USA

South Park
USA, 1997
Trey Parker, Matt Stone

Nickelodeon
USA, 1984
Fred/Alan Inc: Tom Corey, Scott Nash

Animal Planet
USA, 2008
Dunning Eley Jones

Comedy Central
USA, 2000
Imaginary Forces

Sesame Street
USA, 1998

Thomas & Friends
United Kingdom, 2002

Fox Kids
USA

MTV
USA, 1981
Manhattan Design: Pat Gorman,
Frank Olinsky, Patti Rogoff

Divo TV
Russia

Fuji Television Network
Japan

TV Food Network
USA, 1993

13th Street Universal
USA

386

The History Channel
USA, 1995

Turner Classic Movies
(TCM)
USA

Fashion TV
France, 2009

American Movie Classics

AMC
(American Movie Classics)
USA, 2002
Trollbäck & Company

Star Trek – Voyager
USA, 1995

Star Trek – The Next Generation
USA, 1987

Disney Channel
USA, 1987

Disney Channel
USA, 2002
Razorfish

Disney Channel
USA
Razorfish

Discovery Channel
USA, 2009

Discovery Channel
USA, 1987

Travel Channel
USA, 2011
Loyalkaspar

Brand Channel
USA

Travel Channel
United Kingdom, 2000

tiny planets

Tiny Planets
United Kingdom

The Movie Channel
USA, 2006

Global Television Network
Canada

Eurosport
France, 2011

Viasat
Sweden

Sat.1
Germany, 2008

C-SPAN
(Cable-Satellite Public Affairs Network)
USA

RTL 4
Netherlands, 2005

NDR
(Norddeutscher Rundfunk)
Germany, 2001

Star Trek
USA

DirecTV
USA, 2005

Sci-Fi Channel
USA

DSS
(Digital Satellite System)
USA

Dish Network
USA, 2012

ABC
(Australian Broadcasting Corporation)
Australia, 2002

Polskie Radio
Poland, 2004
Studio P: Andrzej Pagowski

Schweizer Fernsehen
Switzerland, 2005
Dunning Eley Jones

Turner
USA, 1987

Cinemax
USA, 2011

Historia
Canada, 2010
Fred Dompierre, Nicolas Ménard

RTL 7
Netherlands, 2010
OOQ

Sun Sports
USA, ca 2004

OLN
Canada, 2011

Fox Sports Net
(FSN)
USA, 2008

Bravo
USA, 2004
Open

Direct 8
France, 2007

BBC
(British Broadcasting Corporation)
United Kingdom, 1997
Martin Lambie-Nairn

RTL
Germany, 1992
GRFX/Novocom

UPN
USA, 1995

TBN
(Trinity Broadcasting Network)
USA

The Box
United Kingdom, 2005

TLC
USA, 2006

Vox
Luxembourg

USA Network
USA, 2005
Peloton Design: Sean Serio

Viva
Germany, 1993

Viva
Germany, 2011
MTV Networks Europe

RT
(Russia Today)
Russia, ca 2009

HLN
(Headline News)
USA, 2008
Digital Kitchen: Brian Bowman, Ben Grube

The Twilight Zone
USA, 1959
Joe Messerli

The Weather Channel
USA

Syfy
USA, 2009
Landor Associates

GSN
USA, 2008
*Buster Design,
Stun Creative*

Film4
United Kingdom, 2006

24
USA, 2001

394

Multicanal

STAR CHANNEL

Multicanal
Argentina, 1996
*Chermayeff & Geismar:
Steff Geissbuhler*

Star Channel
Greece

WE KNOW DRAMA

TNT
(Turner Network Television)
USA, 2008
Troika Design Group

TVR
(Televiziunea Romana)
Romania, 2004
English & Pockett

Telemundo
USA, 1999

RTL Z
Belgium

Fandango
USA

Freesat
United Kingdom

NBC
USA, 1986
Chermayeff & Geismar:
Steff Geissbuhler

CBC
(Canadian Broadcasting Corporation)
Canada, 1992
Gottschalk+Ash

Univision
USA, 1989
Chermayeff & Geismar:
Tom Geismar, Steff Geissbuhler

Astra
Luxembourg

Star Gold
India, 2011

Omni Television
Canada

Knowledge Network
Canada

Bayerischer Rundfunk
(BR)
Germany, 1962
Richard Roth

NBC
USA, 1975

Bayerischer Rundfunk
(BR)
Germany, 1968

Bayerischer Rundfunk
(BR)
Germany, 2007

M6
(Metropole Television)
France

RTL
Netherlands, 2005

TV2
Brazil, 1968
Cauduro Martino

ABC
(Australian Broadcasting Corporation)
Australia, 1975
Bill Kennard

A&E Network
USA

QVC
USA, 2007

DR
(Danmarks Radio)
Denmark, 1964
Connie Linck

WGBH-TV
USA, 1977
Chermayeff & Geismar

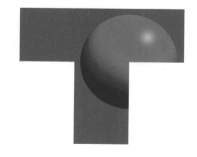

Telemundo
USA, 1992
Chermayeff & Geismar:
Steff Geissbuhler, Robert Matza

ProSieben
Germany, 1994

Channel 5
United Kingdom, 2011

Kanal 5 Danmark
Denmark, 2004

WCVB-TV Channel 5
USA, 1971
*Wyman & Cannon;
Lance Wyman*

5* (Five Star)
United Kingdom, 2011

France 2
France, 2000s

France 3
France, 2000s

Italia 1
Italy

Channel 4
United Kingdom, 2005
Rudd Studio

Who Wants to be a Millionaire?
United Kingdom, 2010

Rede Globo
Brazil, 2008
Hans Donner

American Idol
USA, 2003

Baywatch
USA, 1989

Friends
USA, 1994

The Simpsons
USA, ca 1989
Matt Groening

Spike TV
USA, 2003

Eurovision Song Contest
Switzerland, 2004

Lifetime Television
USA, 2008

The Electric Company
USA

The Green Hornet
USA, 1966

ABC
(American Broadcasting Corporation)
USA, 2007
Troika Design Group

Channel 5
United Kingdom, 1997
Wolff Olins

USSB
(United States
Satellite Broadcasting)
USA, 1996
Paul Rand

Changeman
(Dengeki Sentai
Changeman)
Japan

UPN
USA, 2002

TMC
(Télé Monte Carlo)
France, 2009
Dream On

SRG
Switzerland, 1985

Fox Sports Net
(FSN)
USA, 1999

ZDF
(Zweites Deutsches Fernsehen)
Germany

Cartoon Network
USA, 2010
Brand New School, Cartoon Network

Showtime
USA, 1997
Chermayeff & Geismar

Cinemax
USA, 1997

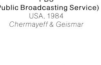

PBS
(Public Broadcasting Service)
USA, 1984
Chermayeff & Geismar

CBS
USA, 1951
William Golden

Comedy Central
USA, 2011
The Lab

Netflix
USA, 1997

CanalSat
France, 2011
Nude

Canal+
France, 1995

TF1
(Télévision Française 1)
France

Cartoon Network
USA, 1992

Stargate SG-1
USA

SRG SSR (Schweizerische Radio- und Fernsehgesellschaft/
Société suisse de radiodiffusion)
Switzerland, 2011
Dunning Penney Jones

Sky Channel
United Kingdom, 2010 Miles Newlyn

TNT
(Turner Network Television)
USA, 1988

ESPN
USA, 1985

CCTV
(Chinese Central Television)
China

CNN
(Cable News Network)
USA, 1980
Toni Dwyer

DD TV
Romania

arte

Arte
France/Germany, 2011

HBO

HBO
USA, 1981

iFC

IFC
(Independent Film Channel)
AMC Networks
USA, 2001

CMT

CMT
USA, 2004

Citytv

Citytv
Canada

starz

Starz
USA
Darwin, Design & Image Communications

Oprah!

Oprah!
USA, 2004

Sony Entertainment Television
USA, 2008

The Box
USA, 1980s

E! Entertainment Television
USA, 1990

MSG Network
USA, 2006

Fine Living
USA, 2002

AMC
(American Movie Classics)
USA, 2007

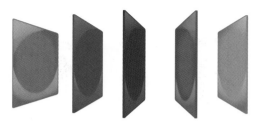

France Télévisions
France, 2008

VH1
USA, 2003

CinéCinéma Channel
France, 2002

FX
USA, 1997

La Sept
(Société d'édition de programmes de télévision)
France, 1989
Étienne Robial, Mathias Ledoux

Interview
USA, 1969
Andy Warhol

PLAYB�eY

Playboy
USA, 1953
Art Paul

Esquire

Esquire
USA

THE NEW YORKER

The New Yorker
USA, 1925
Rea Irvin

the Atlantic

The Atlantic
USA, 2008
*Pentagram: Michael Bierut, Luke Hayman,
Joe Marianek, Ben King*

Fast Company
USA, 1995

Le Progrès
France

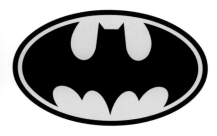

Batman
USA

Superman
USA, 1960s
Curt Swan

Thrasher
USA, 1981

Superman
USA

Asterix
France

Hellboy
USA
Mike Mignola

Action Comics
USA, 1938
Ira R. Schnapp

MAD
USA, ca 1955

People
USA

Vice
Canada/USA

ADWEEK
USA

Ebony
USA

VANITY FAIR

Vanity Fair
USA, 1983

HUSTLER

Hustler
USA, 1974

Dag Allemaal
Netherlands

New York Post
USA

Sports Illustrated
USA

Rolling Stone

Rolling Stone
USA, 1977
Jim Parkinson

Wired
USA, 1994
John Plunkett, Barbara Kuhr

Wired
USA

COSMOPOLITAN

Cosmopolitan
USA

COMPUTERWORLD

Computerworld
USA

Penthouse
USA

All News Channel
USA

GQ
USA, 1990s

FLEX

Flex
USA, 1983

VIBE

Vibe
USA, 1990s

Self
USA

Rocket Comics
USA

Marabout
France

Stern
Germany

Wirtschaftswoche
Germany

New Riders Publishing
USA

Ad Council
USA

NIKKEI

Nikkei
Japan

L'ÉQUIPE

L'Equipe
France

REDBOOK

Redbook
USA

Havas
France

**POPULAR
science**

Popular Science
USA

Cycle World
USA

CINEMANÍA

Cinemanía
Mexico, 2008
La fe ciega studio

REALSIMPLE

Real Simple
USA, 2000

7x7

7x7 San Francisco
USA

BBDO

BBDO
USA, 2012

PCWEEK

PC Week
USA

Las Vegas Magazine
USA, 2006
Pentagram

L!
Lance!
Brazil

Q Magazine
United Kingdom, 1986

Metro International
Luxembourg

Bild
Germany

The Guardian
United Kingdom, 2005
Mark Porter, Paul BarnesChristian Schwartz

Green Lantern
USA

Lowe
United Kingdom, 2003
Carter Wong Tomlin

LA X...Press
USA

Time Out Los Angeles
United Kingdom

Watchmen
USA, 1986

VOGUE

Vogue
USA

TIME

TIME
USA, 1977
Gerard Huerta

ELLE

Elle
France

CONDÉ NAST

Condé Nast
USA

FORTUNE

Fortune
USA

TRIBUNE

Tribune
USA

THE HUFFINGTON POST

The Huffington Post
USA

THE WALL STREET JOURNAL.

The Wall Street Journal
USA

Ms.
USA

U&lc.
(Upper and lower case)
USA, 1973
Herb Lubalin

adforum.com

AdForum
USA

IAB
(Interactive Advertising Bureau)
USA, 2008
Pentagram: Michael Bierut

LA NACION

La Nacion
Argentina, 2000
Rubén Fontana

LE FIGARO

Le Figaro
France

SAATCHI & SAATCHI

Saatchi & Saatchi
United Kingdom
Saatchi & Saatchi

Rotovision
United Kingdom

Modern Times Group
(MTG)
Sweden, 1995

Forbes
USA

Thames & Kosmos
USA, ca 2001

News Corporation
USA

Yellow Pages
USA, 1962
Henry Alexander

La Flor del Itapebi Editorial
Uruguay, 1996
Marcos Larghero

Thames & Hudson
United Kingdom, 1999
The Partners

Playboy
USA, 1953
Art Paul

MIT Press
USA, 1960s
Muriel Cooper

Editorial Andina
Chile, 1974
Mario Fonseca

Maya Ediciones
Ecuador
Azuca Ingenio Gráfico: Diego Corrales

Gotham Books
USA, 2003
Eric Baker, Eric Strohl

Scribner
USA

USA Today
USA, 1982

AFP
France

Chip Magazine
Germany

CIO
USA

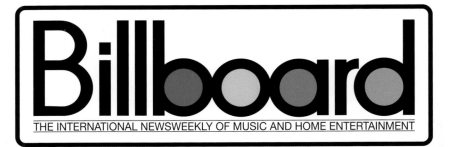

Billboard
USA

Wolters-Noordhoff
Netherlands

Auto Plus
France

Panini Comics
Italy

Yellow Book
USA, 2008

Pearson
United Kingdom

Casterman
Belgium

L'Express
France

Salt Lake City Weekly
USA

LIFE

Life
USA, 1936

Marvel Comics
USA, 2000s

Newsweek
USA
Jim Parkinson

Le Point
France

Big Deal
Belgium

Fooding
France

Paris Match
France, ca 1949

Avenir
France

The Economist
United Kingdom

The Sun
United Kingdom, 1980s

BusinessWeek
USA

SPIN
USA, 1985

Record
Portugal, 2003

News of the World
United Kingdom, 1984

TV Guide
USA, 2003

What's On TV
United Kingdom, 2003

Penguin
United Kingdom, 2005
Pentagram: Angus Hyland

Puffin Books
United Kingdom, 2003
Pentagram

Dark Horse Comics
USA

Hungry Tiger Press
USA

Debrett's
United Kingdom
The Partners

The Black Book
USA

Chronicle Books
USA

Rockport Publishers
USA

Hot Key Books
United Kingdom

FaraEditore
Italy

Röd Press
Sweden

Mondadori Informatica
Italy

Reuters
United Kingdom

Associated Press
USA, 1981

Rogers
Canada

Le Robert
France

France Loisirs
France

Wegener
Netherlands

HarperCollins Publishers
USA
Chermayeff & Geismar

PRINCETON UNIVERSITY PRESS

Princeton University Press
USA, 2007
Chermayeff & Geismar

DC COMICS

DC Comics
USA, 2012
Landor Associates

Taurus Film

Taurus Film
Germany

EMBASSYTELEVISION

Embassy Television
USA, 1982

Gannett
USA, 1979
*Young & Rubicam, Matsuo
Yasamura & Associates*

Cogeco
Canada

GUARDIAN MEDIA GROUP

Guardian Media Group
(GMG)
United Kingdom

428

DC Comics
USA, 1976
Milton Glaser

Le Livre de Poche
France

Lonely Planet
Australia

Eye
The International Review of Graphic Design
United Kingdom

Primedia
South Africa

Que Publishing
USA

Dragon Ball Z
Japan
Funimation Productions

DC Comics
USA, 2005
Brainchild Studios: Josh Beatman

Y&R
(Young & Rubicam)
USA

Dorling Kindersley (DK)
United Kingdom, 2003
Pentagram

Delcourt
France

Libération
France

The New York Times Company
USA

Le Monde

Le Monde
France

Aftenposten

Aftenposten
Norway

The Washington Post

The Washington Post
USA

The Daily Telegraph

The Daily Telegraph
Australia

The New York Times

The New York Times
USA

Los Angeles Times

Los Angeles Times
USA

Chicago Tribune

Chicago Tribune
USA

FoodBusiness*news*

FoodBusiness News
USA

THE Daily Telegraph

The Daily Telegraph
United Kingdom

la Repubblica

La Repubblica
Italy, ca 1976

MarketingWeek

Marketing Week
United Kingdom

Bloomberg

Bloomberg
USA

InfoWorld

InfoWorld
USA

MacWEEK

MacWEEK
USA

Mademoiselle

Mademoiselle
USA

Macworld

Macworld
USA, 1990s

432

Fixot
France

Faber and Faber
United Kingdom
Pentagram

Little Brown & Company
USA, 2009
Lance Hidy

Gruner + Jahr
Germany

Andrews McMeel Universal
USA, 1985
Chermayeff & Geismar: Steff Geissbuhler

Hachette Livre
France

Peace Symbol
United Kingdom, 1958
Gerald Holtom

LOVE
USA, 1964
Robert Indiana

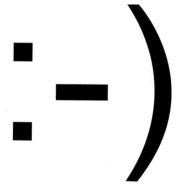

Digital Emoticon
USA, 1982
Scott Fahlman

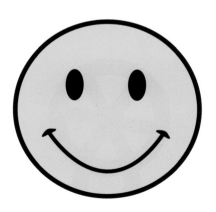

Smiley
USA, 1963
Harvey Ball

Ministry of Sound
United Kingdom, 1991
Marc Woodhouse, Justin Berkman

COMTEK
Russia, 2003

Marcus Theatres
USA

Bundesgartenschau
Germany
Helmut Langer

**4th Centenary of the
City of Rio de Janeiro**
Brazil, 1964
Aloísio Magalhães

Volksbühne
Germany, 1992
Bert Neumann

National Arts Centre
Canada, 1967
Design Collaborative

Palace Amusement Co. (1921) Ltd
Jamaica

Fida Film
Turkey

Village Cinemas
Australia

UGC Cinémas
France

VIV América Latina
Netherlands

TED
(Technology Entertainment and Design)
USA

Miss America
USA

NetWorld Interop
USA

AMC Theatres
(American Multi-Cinema)
USA

Ro Theater
Netherlands, 2009
75B

Jarman Award
United Kingdom, 2009
KentLyons: Jon Cefai

Greater Union
Australia

Madison Square Garden
USA

Fil
(Festival Intercâmbio de Linguagens)
Brazil, 2008
Laboratório Secreto: Marcelo Martinez

National Theatre
United Kingdom, 1971
Ian Dennis, FHK Henrion

Cineworld
United Kingdom, 2009

The Public Theater
USA, 2008
Pentagram: Paula Scher

Mind the Gap
United Kingdom
Brahm

New York City Ballet
USA, 2008
Pentagram: Paula Scher

Wembley Stadium
United Kingdom, 2010
Bulletproof

Rockefeller Center
USA, 1985
Chermayeff & Geismar

New National Theatre Tokyo
Japan

The Kennedy Center
USA

Toronto Zoo
Canada, 2004
Hambly & Woolley: Barbara Woolley

SeaWorld
USA

Holiday on Ice
Netherlands

Los Angeles Zoo
USA

Miss Universe
USA

Lisbon Aquarium
Portugal, 1998
Chermayeff & Geismar

ISLAND

Island Records
USA

GEFFEN

Geffen Records
USA, 1980
Saul Bass

EMI-CAPITOL MUSIC

EMI-Capitol Music
USA

Hollywood Records
USA, 1995

SONY MUSIC

Sony Music
USA, 2009

Abbey Road Studios
United Kingdom
Ed Lea

Gibson
USA, ca 1947

Fender
USA

Epic Records
USA, ca 1992

Pathé Records
France, 1900s

Marshall
United Kingdom, 1960s

Capitol Records
USA

Warp Records
United Kingdom, 1989
The Designers Republic: Ian Anderson

Labrador Records
Sweden

Gig Ant Promotion
Poland

Fox Records
USA, 1990s

RIAA
USA

RCA Records
USA, 1988

Verve
USA, 1956

Epic Records
USA, 1979

Epic Records
USA, 1970s

Evans Drumheads
USA

Rhino Records
USA

Virgin Records
United Kingdom

Wall of Sound
United Kingdom

Uni Records
USA, 1967

United Artists Records
USA, ca 1970

Mercury Records
United Kingdom

Jive Records
USA

4AD
United Kingdom, ca 1983
V23: Vaughan Oliver

Choice Records
France, 2000
H5: Ludovic Houplain

Warner Music Group
USA, 1972
Saul Bass

English National Opera
United Kingdom, 1991
CDT: Mike Dempsey

Elektra Records
USA

V2 Music
United Kingdom

Reprise Records
USA, 1960s

American Recording
USA

Bands of America
USA

Tama Drums
Japan, ca 1974

ARP
USA, 1970s

Motor
Germany

Fog City Records
USA

The Who
United Kingdom, 1964
Brian Pike

The Rolling Stones
United Kingdom, 1971
John Pasche

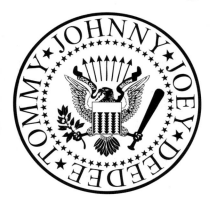

Ramones
USA, 1970s
Arturo Vega

Red Hot Chilli Peppers
USA
Anthony Kiedis

448

Van Halen
USA, 1978
Dave Bhang

Linkin Park
USA

Danko Jones
Canada

AC/DC
Australia, 1977
Gerard Huerta

Kiss
USA, 1973
Ace Frehley

Groove Armada
United Kingdom
Zip

The Clash
United Kingdom, ca 1977

Metallica
USA, 1980s
James Hetfield

Björk
United Kingdom, 1990s

Aerosmith
USA, 1971
Ray Tabano

Walt Disney Records
USA

RCA
(Nipper the dog)
USA, 1977

Duck Records
United Kingdom, ca 1982

His Master's Voice
(HMV)
United Kingdom, 2007

Motown Records
USA

STEINWAY & SONS

Steinway
USA

The Met
ropolitan
Opera

The Metropolitan Opera
USA, 2006
Pentagram: Paula Scher, Julia Hoffmann

ATLANTIC

Atlantic Records
USA, 2005

Queen
United Kingdom, 1970s
Freddie Mercury

NIRVANA

Nirvana
USA, 1989
Lisa Orth

Run D.M.C.
USA

Elektra Records
USA

NIN
(Nine Inch Nails)
USA, 1989
Trent Reznor, Gary Talpas

Muse
United Kingdom, 1998

Atlantic Records
USA, 1966

Polydor Records
Germany

Edel Music
Germany

Motown Records
USA, 1965

Epic Records
USA, 1960s

A&M Records
USA, 1962

Sony Music
USA

Oasis
United Kingdom, 1994
Microdot Creative: Brian Cannon

EMI
United Kingdom

The Beatles
United Kingdom, 1963
Ivor Arbiter

Sex Pistols
United Kingdom, 1976
Jamie Reid

Pulp
United Kingdom

Whitesnake
United Kingdom
Jim Gibson

The Chemical Brothers
United Kingdom

Daft Punk
France, 1997
Guy-Manuel de Homem-Christo

Gorillaz

Gorillaz
United Kingdom, 1998
Jamie Hewlett

Fatboy Slim
United Kingdom

Looptroop Rockers
Sweden

Fiction Records
United Kingdom

Cypress Hill
USA, ca 2001

Public Enemy
USA, 1986
Carlton Douglas Ridenhour (aka Chuck D)

Wu Tang Clan
USA
Allah Mathematics

For us the living
USA

Eagle Records
United Kingdom

Factory Records
United Kingdom, ca 1978
Peter Saville

Pump Records
USA

Sire Records
USA, 1960s

Diamondtraxx
France
H5: Yorgo Tloupas

Legacy Recordings
USA, 1990

Behringer
Germany

Westbound
USA
SightTwo

Labels
France

456

Ninja Tune Records
United Kingdom, ca 1994
Kevin Foakes

Naked Music
USA

Source Records
France, 2006
M/M Paris

Green Day
American Idiot
USA, 2004
Chris Bilheimer

Epic Records
USA, 2011

Ibanez Guitars
Japan

Pearl
Japan

Wenger
USA

Moog Music
USA

Buzzcocks
United Kingdom, 1977
Malcolm Garrett

WEA
(Warner-Elektra-Atlantic)
USA

RCA
USA, 1969

Abba
Sweden, 1976
Rune Söderqvist

Korg
Japan

Vertigo
United Kingdom, 1969
Linda Glover

I.R.S. Records
(International Record Syndicate)
USA, 1979

Meinl Percussion
Germany

Massive Music
Netherlands

Roland
Japan

Boss
Japan, 1973

Rammstein
Germany, 2001
Dirk Rudolph

SERVICE & BUSINESS

AIRLINES
AUCTIONING & AUDITING
CATERING
CONSULTANCY
ENERGY
HEALTH SERVICES
HOSPITALITY
LOGISTICS
OUTSOURCING
PHARMACEUTICAL
PRINTING SERVICES
SECURITY SERVICES
TELECOMMUNICATIONS
TRANSPORT
UTILITY COMPANIES

MTA New York City Transit
USA

Underground
United Kingdom, ca 1919
Edward Johnston

S-Bahn
Germany, 1930s

S-Bahn
Austria

British Rail
United Kingdom, 1965
Design Research Unit:
Gerry Barney

Montreal Metro/
Métro de Montréal
Canada

Nederlandse Spoorwegen
Netherlands, 1968
Gert Dumbar, Gert-Jan Leuvelink

Tokyu Corporation
Japan

Norbert Dentressangle
France

One
United Kingdom, 2004
Lawrence Pierce

Russian Railways
Russia, 2007

Via
Canada

GATX Corporation
USA

AEI
USA

CN
(Canadian National Railway)
Canada, 1960
Allan Fleming

JR
(Japan Rail)
Japan

VR
Finland, 2009

IER
France

SNCF
(Société Nationale des Chemins de fer français)
France, 1986
Roger Tallon

SNCF
(Société Nationale des Chemins de fer français)
France, 2005
Carré Noir

DB
(Deutsche Bahn)
Germany, 1993
Kurt Weidemann

Yellow Freight
USA

Penske
USA

QR (Queensland Rail)
Australia, 2010
Cornwall Design

Burlington Northern Railroad
USA

Mexico City Metro
Mexico, 1969
Lance Wyman

Amtrak
USA, 2000
OH&CO: Brent Oppenheimer

Eurostar
United Kingdom, 2011
SomeOne

Amtrak
USA, 1971
Lippincott & Margulies

DSB (Danske Statsbaner)
Denmark

STM
(Société de transport de Montréal/
Montreal Transit Corporation)
Canada, 2009
Sid Lee

STCP
(Sociedade de Transportes
Colectivos do Porto)
Portugal

Stagecoach Group
United Kingdom

Roads Service
United Kingdom

SBB CFF FFS
(Schweizerische Bundesbahnen)
Switzerland, 1978
Josef Müller-Brockmann, Peter Spalinger

Nippon Express
Japan

CityBus
China

SNCM
(Société Nationale Maritime
Corse Méditerranée)
France

FirstGroup
United Kingdom

Lachmann
Brazil
Ana Couto Branding & Design

Heidmar
USA

GVB Amsterdam
Netherlands, 1970

Nedlloyd
Netherlands

KMB
(Kowloon Motor Bus)
China

Autoroutes du Sud de la France
(ASF)
France

RATP Group
(Régie Autonome des Transports Parisiens)
France

Renfe
Spain, 1972

VTG-Lehnkering AG
Germany

AHI
USA

Caltrans
USA, 1973
Dave Douglas

Rex Regional Express
Australia, 2002

Coach USA
USA

Offshore Logistics Inc
USA

C.H. Robinson Worldwide Inc
USA

North American
USA

Calberson
France

Demeco
France

Stena
Sweden

Greyhound Lines
USA

Indian Pacific
Australia

Helicraft
Canada

Idealease
USA

Cosco Pacific
China

Odyssey
Russia

DoKaSch
Germany

Acciona Airport Services
Spain

AccesRail
Canada

TDG
United Kingdom

Global Van Lines
USA

Rush
USA

Union Pacific
USA, 1969

Acela Express
USA, 2000
OH&CO, IDEO

CityRail
Australia, 2010

National Express
United Kingdom

THALES

Thales
France, 2000
Euro RSCG

VR CARGO

VR Cargo
Finland

Scottish Citylink
United Kingdom

Allied Van Lines
USA

Hertz Rent-A-Car
USA, 2009
Landor Associates

Avis Rent a Car
USA

Europcar
France

National Car Rental
USA

Enterprise Rent-A-Car
USA, 2010

Alamo
USA

Hertz Rent-A-Car
USA, 1978

Sixt
Germany

Cruise America
USA

Advantage Rent-a-Car
USA

Exel
USA, 1992

Exel
USA, 2000

Dollar Rent A Car
USA

XTRA Corporation
USA

Driving Force
Canada

Budget Rent A Car
USA

Saudi Arabian Airlines
Saudi Arabia, 2006

Air Madagascar
Madagascar, 2004
Peter Schmidt Group

Air Jamaica
Jamaica/Trinidad and Tobago

Canadian Airlines
Canada, 1999
Landor Associates

Air India
India, 2007

AeroMéxico
Mexico

Jet Aviation
Switzerland

EgyptAir
Egypt

Olympic Airways
Greece, 1960s

virgin atlantic

Virgin Atlantic Airways
United Kingdom, 2010
johnson banks, Virgin Atlantic

go

Go Airlines
United Kingdom, 1998
Wolff Olins: Joseph Mitchell

vueling

Vueling
Spain, 2004
Saffron Brand Consultants

VARIG

Varig
Brazil, 2007

United Airlines
USA, 1974
Saul Bass

TAP

TAP Portugal
Portugal

Delta Airlines
USA, 2000
Landor Associates

DELTA

Delta Airlines
USA, 2007
Lippincott Mercer

 Condor

Condor Flugdienst
Germany

Lufthansa

Lufthansa
Germany, 1969
Otl Aicher

 LUXAIR

Luxair
Luxembourg

Martinair

Martinair
Netherlands

Swiss International Airlines
Switzerland, 2011

THAI

Thai Airways
Thailand, 2005
Interbrand

Singapore Airlines
Singapore

Shuttle by United
USA, 1990s

Comair
USA

Brussels Airlines
Belgium, 2007
Hoet & Hoet

Niki
Austria

Flybe
United Kingdom, 2004

AirAsia
Malaysia

Aloha Airlines
USA

Alaska Airlines
USA

QATAR AIRWAYS القطرية

Qatar Airways
Qatar, 2006

Gulf Air
Bahrain

BRITISH AIRWAYS

British Airways
United Kingdom, 1997
Interbrand Newell & Sorrell

British Airways
United Kingdom, 1984
Landor Associates

Continental

Continental Airlines
USA, 1991
Lippincott & Margulies

airJamaica

Air Jamaica
Jamaica/Trinidad and Tobago
Stewart & Morrison: Hans Kleefeld

PIA
Pakistan International

Pakistan International Airlines
(PIA)
Pakistan

BAA

BAA
(British Airport Authority)
United Kingdom, 1986
Lloyd Northover

Air China
China, 1988
Shao Xin, Han Meilin

Aerolíneas Argentinas
Argentina, 2010
FutureBrand

DutchBird
Netherlands, 2000

Neos
Italy

Eva Air
Taiwan

Finnair
Finland, 2010
SEK & Grey

Czech Airlines
(CSA)
Czech Republic

Midwest Airlines
USA

TACA Airlines
(Transportes Aéreos del Continente Americano)
El Salvador, 2008
Lippincott

Turkish Airlines
Turkey, 2010

TACA Airlines
(Transportes Aéreos del Continente Americano)
El Salvador

Iceland Express
Iceland

Jet Airways
India, 1993
Lintas: KV Sridhar (mark)

Sabena
Belgium

Jetset Travel
Australia

AIR FRANCE

Air France
France, 1975

AIRFRANCE

Air France
France, 2009
Brandimage

ICELANDAIR

Icelandair
Iceland

Garuda Indonesia

Garuda Indonesia
Indonesia, 2009

RYANAIR

Ryanair
Ireland

FINNAIR

Finnair
Finland, 2000
SEK & Grey

KOREAN AIR

Korean Air
South Korea

Alitalia

Alitalia
Italy, 2005

USAir

USAir
USA, 1989
SBG Partners

Lacsa

Lacsa
Costa Rica

AIR NEW ZEALAND

Air New Zealand
New Zealand, 2006

SOUTH AFRICAN AIRWAYS

South African Airways
South Africa

Air India
India, 1948

SINGAPORE AIRLINES

Singapore Airlines
Singapore, 1987

Monarch

Monarch
United Kingdom, 1980s

cargolux

Cargolux
Luxembourg

BERJAYA

Berjaya Air
Malaysia

JAL
(Japan Airlines)
Japan, 2011

Pan Am
USA

KLM Royal Dutch Airlines
Netherlands, 1991
Henrion, Ludlow & Schmidt: Chris Ludlow

Emirates Airlines
United Arab Emirates, 1999

S7 Airlines
Russia, 2005
Landor Associates

Aeroperu
Peru

DragonAir
China, 1985

Aer Lingus
Ireland

Air Canada
Canada, 2004
FutureBrand: Claude Salzberger

Hawaiian Arlines
USA, 1993
Lindon Leader

STAR ALLIANCE

Star Alliance
Germany

SkyTeam
Netherlands

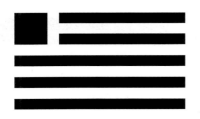

US Airways
USA, 1997
Deskey Associates: Luxon Carrá

SAS
Sweden, 1998
Stockholm Design Lab, TEArk

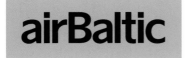

airBaltic
Latvia, 2004

EasyJet
United Kingdom, 1995

Swiss International Airlines
Switzerland, 2002
Winkreative

Iberia Airlines
Spain

TWA (Trans World Airlines)
USA
Raymond Loewy

Kuoni
Switzerland

Thomas Cook
United Kingdom, 2001

FRONTIER AIRLINES

Frontier Airlines
USA

jetBlue
AIRWAYS

JetBlue Airways
USA, 2009

SkyWest
AIRLINES

SkyWest Airlines
USA

The Emirates Group

Emirates Group
United Arab Emirates, 1999

Fly Emirates

Fly Emirates
United Arab Emirates

bmi
(British Midland International)
United Kingdom

LOT Polish Airlines
Poland, 1978
Roman Duszek, Andrzej Zbrozek

Aeroflot
Russia

Qantas
Australia, 2008

American Airlines
USA, 1967
Massimo Vignelli

Sata International
Portugal

IranAir
Iran, 1962

TUI
Germany, 2001
Interbrand Zintzmeyer & Lux

GO Voyages
France

CPH
Denmark

Silja Line
Finland

Fram
France

Royal Caribbean International
Norway/USA

United States Lines
USA

Selectour Voyages
France

City Hopper
United Kingdom, 2006
ICG

Dubai Ports Authority
United Arab Emirates

P&O Cruises
United Kingdom/USA

Toronto Pearson Greater
Canada, 2011

Majesty Cruise Line
Norway

Cunard Line
United Kingdom

Hurricane

Hurricane
United Kingdom

Gazprom
Russia

Galp Energia
Portugal, 2003

PEMEX
Mexico, 1989

Tatneft
Russia

PECO Energy
USA

Dominion
USA

Cosmo Oil
Japan

Conelsur
Chile, 2007
Grupo Oxigeno

Exxon
USA, 1972
Raymond Loewy

AGA
Finland

Cinergy
USA

Questar
USA, 1998

NTPC
(National Thermal Power Corporation)
India

Dyneff
France, 2008

Statoil
Norway

Arco
USA

Vattenfall
Sweden

British Gas
United Kingdom, 2012
CHI & Partners

Energy Trust
USA

Erdgas/Natural Gas
Switzerland

Natural Gas
Switzerland

Devon
USA

Dynegy
USA
Will Ayres

Suncor Energy
Canada

Unocal
(Union Oil Company of California)
USA

DEA
(Deutsche Erdöl AG)
Germany

Petronas
Malaysia

Lukoil
Russia

Duke Energy
USA

conEdison
USA, 2000
Arnell Group

J-Power
Japan

Petro Rabigh
Saudi Arabia, 2007

Delta Electricity
Australia

Statoil
Norway, 2009
Scandinavian Design Group

Shell
Netherlands/United Kingdom, 1971
Raymond Loewy

Total
France, 2003
A&Co Paris: Laurent Vincenti

**Petróleos de Venezuela
(PDVSA)**
Venezuela, 1975
Jesús Emilio Franco

São Paulo Petróleo
Brazil, 1986
Alexandre Wollner

**Callon Petroleum
Company**
USA

Detroit Diesel
USA

BP
United Kingdom, 2000
Landor Associates

Chevron
USA, 1960s
Lippincott & Margulies: Raymond Poelvoorde

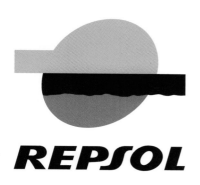

REPJOL

Repsol
Spain

PetroChina

PetroChina
China, 2004

PECSA

PECSA
Peru

Slovnaft

Slovnaft
Slovakia

CΛLTEX

Caltex
USA, ca 1987

PETRO·CANADA

Petro-Canada
Canada
Interbrand

CITGO

Citgo
USA, 1965
Lippincott & Margulies

TEXACO

Texaco
USA, 1981

494

PO (Petrol Ofisi)
Turkey

Sonangol
Angola, 2004

Sinclair
USA

CEA (Commissariat
Energie Atomique)
France

Rheem
USA

Full
Argentina, 2005
Rubén Fontana

Tenneco
USA, 1995
Lippincott & Margulies

Marathon
USA

Gulf Oil
USA, 1960

Fina
Belgium, 1972

Oxy Petroleum
USA

76
USA

Petroplus
Switzerland

Esso
USA, 1923

Petrobras
Brazil, 1970
Aloísio Magalhães

CEPSA
(Compañía Española de Petróleos SA)
Spain

Hess
USA

AKSA Energy
Turkey

Petrom
Romania

Ultramar
Canada

Light
Brazil, 1998
eg.design

AGIP
(Azienda Generale Italiana Petroli)
Italy, 1998
Unimark: Bob Noorda

Kerr-McGee
USA

Naftal Algerie
Algeria

Canadian Natural
Canada

Orlen
Poland, 2000
Henryk Chylinski

Nippon Sanso
Japan

Hercules Offshore
USA

Diamond Shamrock
USA

**Enterprise
Products Partners**
USA

Engen
South Africa

Tenneco
USA, 1990s
Lippincott & Margulies

Sunoco
USA, ca 2000

Williams
USA

Ultragaz
Brazil, 1977
Alexandre Wollner

SOCAR
Azerbaijan

Carrier
USA

ESB
Ireland

Bryant
USA

Goodman Manufacturing
USA

Thames Water
United Kingdom

Payne
USA

GAF
USA

Shaw
USA

Deceuninck
Belgium

Siebe
United Kingdom

e.on
Germany

Oxxio
Netherlands

Totaline
USA

Hilti
Liechtenstein, 2005
NVA Studio

FIREloc
USA

Grupo Prasa
Spain

Pacific Gas and Electric Company
(PG&E)
USA

Gaz de France
France, 1987

HEIDELBERG Technology
Germany

VIESSMANN

Viessman
Germany, 1960
Stankowski & Duschek: Anton Stankowski

ruukki

Ruukki
Finland

uponor

Uponor
Finland

SCHÜCO

Schüco
Germany, 2003
Peter Schmidt Group

VOGELZANG

Vogelzang
USA

FEDDERS

Fedders
USA

SKANSKA

Skanska
Sweden

Vickers
United Kingdom

Hazama

Hazama Corporation
Vietnam

Frico
Sweden

IMI International
Spain

Tempstar
USA

ComEd
USA

MASCO

Masco
USA

Danfoss
Denmark

Southern Californian Gas Company
(SoCalGas)
USA

California Water Service Co.
USA

502

Commsa
Mexico

Veolia
France, 2005

Elco
Greece

Idacorp
USA

Yonden
Japan, ca 1991

TEPCO
Japan

 FURNAS

Furnas
Brazil

Westinghouse
USA, 1960
Paul Rand

 COPEL

Copel
(Companhia Paranaense de Energia)
Brazil

 Strukton

Strukton
Netherlands

Fortum
Finland

TXU Energy
USA, 2010

United Utilities
United Kingdom

Northeast Utilities System
USA

Point.P
France

Peoples Energy
USA

RWE

RWE
Germany, 2008
Jung von Matt

Gaz de France

Gaz de France
France

Southern Company
USA
Lippincott

energie thun

Energie Thun
Switzerland

TOKYO GAS

Tokyo Gas
Japan

gasNatural
fenosa

Gas Natural Fenosa
Spain, 2010

eDF
ENERGY

EDF
France, 2005
*Plan Créatif: Vanessa van Steelandt,
Patrick Le Mahec, Sophie Tchérakian*

SDGE
(San Diego Gas & Electric)
USA

LP
(Louisiana-Pacific)
USA, 1973

Todini
Italy

American States
WATER COMPANY

American States
Water Company
USA

Faber Bygg A.S.
Norway

ScottishPower
United Kingdom, 1990

United Utilities
United Kingdom

FRESHFIELDS BRUCKHAUS DERINGER

Freshfields Bruckhaus Deringer
United Kingdom, 2000
Gottschalk+Ash

Getinge
Sweden

Grant Thornton
United Kingdom, 2008
Pentagram: Angus Hyland

Ernst & Young
United Kingdom

ISS
(International Service System)
United Kingdom

CHEP
(Commonwealth Handling
Equipment Pool Organisation)
Australia

Aramark
USA, 1994
Schecter Interbrand

Aegis Communications
India

Falck
Denmark

Fastsigns
USA

Sodexo
France, 2008
W&Cie

CWS
Germany

Viking
USA

KPMG
Netherlands
Interbrand

Brinks
USA

INCM
Portugal

Gelco
(General Equipment
Leasing Corporation)
USA

Bowne
USA

Secom
Japan

508

Geobrugg
Switzerland

OCTANORM✿

Octanorm
Germany

Cramo
Finland

SERVPRO®

Servpro
USA

ABUS
Germany

Danko Emergency
Equipment
USA

MSA
(Mine Safety Appliance)
USA

GALLUP

Gallup
USA

Precision Locker
USA

Quik Print
USA

accenture

Accenture
Ireland, 2001
Landor Associates

Letraset

Letraset
United Kingdom

Deloitte.

Deloitte
United Kingdom
The Brand Union

Algeco
France

KINTEK

Kintek
Italy

M RNINGSTAR

Morningstar
USA, 1991
Paul Rand

Brinks
USA

ADT Security Services
Switzerland

Atlas Fence
USA

G&K Services
USA

SAI Global
Australia

General Monitors
USA

Orkin
USA

Fireye
USA

Millward Brown
United Kingdom

Osuna Nursery
USA

Graham
USA

ISS
Denmark

Adecco
Switzerland

Securitas
Sweden

Foex
Finland

Depom
Turkey

Säkerhetspartner
Sweden

Thomson
France

Securitas
Switzerland

DiamondCluster
USA

Republic Services
USA

Safescan
Netherlands

Moore Wallace

Moore Wallace
USA

Manpower

Manpower
USA, 2006
Wolff Olins: Luke Gifford

REED

Reed
United Kingdom

MLC Services
United Kingdom, ca 2006

flyerwire.de
Germany

Gateway Safety Inc
USA

Babcock
United Kingdom

novo nordisk

Novo Nordisk
Denmark

TM

MILLIPORE

Millipore
USA, 2011

BOOTS HEALTHCARE
INTERNATIONAL

Boots Healthcare International
United Kingdom

WYETH LEDERLE

Wyeth Lederle
USA

SB
SmithKline Beecham

Smithkline Beecham
United Kingdom

Banner Health

Banner Health
USA

MYLAN

Mylan Inc
USA

KYOWA

Kyowa
Japan

US Oncology

US Oncology
USA

DentsCare

DentsCare
Brazil

Cigna
USA, 2011
BrandSinger, Jerry Kuyper Partners

The Children's Medical Center
USA

Premier Research Group
USA

InfantSEE
USA

National Blood Service
United Kingdom

Servior
Luxembourg

Unimed
Brazil

PHARMACIA

Pharmacia
United Kingdom, 2000
Landor Associates

McKESSON

McKesson
USA

SUCRETS

Sucrets
USA

PAREXEL

Parexel
USA

Dristan

Dristan
USA

Genentech

Genentech
USA

TaKaRa

Takara Bio
Japan

Maalox

Maalox
Switzerland

AMGEN

Amgen
USA

ACTIFED

Actifed
USA

ACUVUE

Acuvue
USA

Visine
USA

DaVita
USA, 2003
IE Design + Communications

Vivantes
Germany, 2006
Pentagram

UpJohn
USA

NHS

NHS (National Health Service)
United Kingdom, 1990
Moon Brand: Richard Moon

Toothfriendly
International
Switzerland

Cardinal Health
USA

Abacus International
Singapore, 2006
Unreal

Advil
USA

Aleve
USA
Szylinski Associates

TAP Pharmaceuticals
USA

UCB Pharma
(Union Chimique Belge)
Belgium

WeightWatchers

WeightWatchers
USA

blue of california

Blue Shield of California
USA

TAISHO PHARMACEUTICAL CO., LTD.

Taisho Pharmaceutical
Japan

AstraZeneca

AstraZeneca
United Kingdom, 1999
Interbrand Newell & Sorrell

Anda

UPSA Laboratories
France

Anda
USA, ca 1992

Pfizer
USA, 2009
Siegel+Gale

Roche
Switzerland

Wick
Germany, 2008

Knoll
Germany

Merz
Germany

Bayer
Germany, 2002
Claus Koch

Abbott Laboratories
USA

Arcares
Netherlands

Takeda
Japan

Vicks
USA

Schering-Plough
USA

McKesson HBOC
USA

Leiner
USA

Datex Ohmeda
USA

Johnson & Johnson
USA, 1886
James Wood Johnson

Lilly
USA

Wyeth
USA, 2002
Landor Associates

DAK
Germany

MET-Rx
USA

Supra Vit
Bulgaria

Circle
United Kingdom

Merck
Germany

Aventis
France, 1999
Corporate Branding

Amersham
United Kingdom, 2001
Wolff Olins

Fresenius Medical Care
USA

GSK
United Kingdom, 2001
FutureBrand

Yamanouchi
Japan

Suzuken
Japan

Allergan
USA

Bristol-Myers Squibb
USA, ca 1989

Maret
USA

GN ReSound Group
Denmark

Boehringer Ingelheim
Germany, 1997
MetaDesign: Ole Schäfer

Nuvelo
USA

Merck
USA, 1991
Chermayeff & Geismar:
Audrey Kraus, Steff Geissbuhler

Warner Chilcott
Ireland

Ibis Hotels
France, 2011
W&Cie

Best Western
USA, 1993

ETAP Accor Hotels
France, 1996

Hampton
USA

Wingate Inn
USA
Lippincott

Days Inn
USA, 2007

Country Inns & Suites
USA

Residence Inn by Marriott
USA

Tokyu Hotels
Japan

La Quinta Inn
USA

Budget Host Inn
USA

Holiday Inn Express
United Kingdom, 2007
Interbrand

Super 8 Motels
USA, 2008

Super 8 Motels
USA, 1982

All Seasons Hotels
France, 2011
W&Cie

Holiday Inn
USA, 2007

Comfort Inn
USA

Comfort Suites
USA

Sleep Inn
USA

Motel 6
USA/Canada

Clarion Hotels
USA

Red Lion Hotels
USA

Campanile

Campanile
France

nikko hotels
international

Nikko Hotels International
Japan

InterContinental Hotels
United Kingdom

Wyndham Hotels & Resorts
USA

Red Roof Inn
USA

Knights Inn
USA

Radisson Hotels
USA

Hyatt
USA, 1990
Landor Associates

21c Museum Hotel
USA, 2006
Pentagram

Rhiga Royal Hotels
Japan

MGM Grand
USA

Tropical
Brazil, 1966
Ruben Martins

CONRAD
HOTELS

Conrad Hotels
USA

SOFITEL

Sofitel
France

W Hotels
USA, 1990s

Hilton Hotels & Resorts
USA, 1998
Enterprise IG: Gene Grossman

The Dorchester Collection
United Kingdom, 2006
Pentagram: John Rushworth

Faena
Argentina, 2004
Tholön Kunst

530

Homewood Suites
USA

Deer Valley Resort
Germany

MGM Grand
USA

Ritz Carlton Hotels
USA
Cesar Ritz

Omni Hotels
USA

Oakwood
USA

Marriott
USA

Club Med
France

Park Inn
USA, 2010

Motel One
Germany

Accor
France

HomeAway
USA

Sheraton Hotels & Resorts
USA

Center Parcs
Netherlands, 1997

Huawei
China, 2006

AT&T
USA, 1983
Yager & Associates:
Saul Bass, Jerry Kuyper

Boost Mobile
USA, 2008
Attik

Vodavi
USA

Eircom
Ireland

Swisscom
Switzerland, 2008
Moving Brands

Alcatel-Lucent
France, 2006
Landor Associates

Sony Ericsson
United Kingdom, 2001
Takuya Kawagoi

Lucent Technologies
USA

Bouygues Telecom
France

Telecom New Zealand
New Zealand, 2009
Designworks

France Telecom
France, 2000
Landor Associates

China Unicom
China, 2006

NorthwesTel
USA

NTT Communications
Corporation
Japan

China Mobile 3G
China, 2009

Vodafone
United Kingdom, 2005
Enterprise IG

Vodafone
United Kingdom, 1997
Saatchi & Saatchi

Three
United Kingdom

KPN
Netherlands, 2006
Studio Dumbar

Bell Canada
Canada, 1994
Bell Canada

WorldCom
USA, 2000
Interbrand

TM Telekom Malaysia
Malaysia

MCI Worldcom
USA, 1995/2003
Interbrand

Telecom Italia
Italy, 2003

Swisscom
Switzerland, 1997

KPN
Netherlands, 2004
Studio Dumbar

Orange
France, 1994
Wolff Olins

GTL
India

MTC
India

Benefon
Finland

Ferma
France

Telcel
Mexico

Cable & Wireless Worldwide
United Kingdom, 2010
TBD

Mitel Networks
Canada

SAGEM
(Société d'Applications Générales de
l'Électricité et de la Mécanique)
France

Comcast
USA, 2007

Farallon Computing
USA

France Telecom
France

US Cellular
USA

Telekom Srbija
Serbia, ca 1997

Global Crossing
Bermuda

Batelco
Bahrain, 2010
FutureBrand

Batelco
Bahrain, 2010
FutureBrand

O2
United Kingdom, 2002
Lambie-Nairn

Telekom Deutschland
Germany
Interbrand

Bell System
USA, 1921

Bell System
USA, 1964

Perumtel
Indonesia, 1974

C-Netz
Germany, 1984

Bell System
USA, 1969
Saul Bass & Associates

Claro
Brazil, 2006
GAD

BT Group
United Kingdom, 2003
Wolff Olins

NET
Brazil

NetCologne

NetCologne
Germany

Allied Data Technologies
Netherlands

Cingular
USA, 2000
VSA Partners

T-Mobile
Germany, 1993
Interbrand Zintzmeyer & Lux

Telewest
United Kingdom, 1980s

China Telecom
China

Tellabs
USA

VTR
Chile

Cable & Wireless Communications
United Kingdom, 2010
Elmwood

Motorola
USA, 1955
Zeke Ziner

Telenor
Norway, 2006
Wolff Olins: Keshen Teo

Airtel
India, 2010
The Brand Union

EMBARQ

Embarq
USA, 2006

djuice

djuice
Norway, 2006
Wolff Olins

freenet

Freenet
Germany

SHAW

Shaw Communications
Canada, 1997

United Telecom

United Telecom
USA, ca 1972

ERICSSON

Ericsson
Sweden, 1982
AID: Terry Moore

ED TEL

Ed Tel
(Edmonton Telephones Corporation)
Canada

TELE2

Tele2
Sweden, 2007

Telekom Slovenije
Republic of Slovenia

Telkom Indonesia
Indonesia, 2009

Sprint
USA, 2005
Lippincott Mercer

Qwest
USA, 1998
Enterprise IG

VolgaTelecom
Russia, 2002

SBC
USA, 1995

TIM
(Telecom Italia Mobile)
Italy, 2016
Interbrand

Joe Mobile
France, 2012

TIM
(Telecom Italia Mobile)
Italy

Telfort
Netherlands, 2010
VBAT

DNA
Finland

GTE Corporation
USA

djuice
Norway

Hi
Netherlands

1&1 Ionos
Germany

Oi
Brazil, 2001
WolffOllins

Telfort.

Telfort
Netherlands, 1996

Telefónica

Telefónica
Spain, 1998
FutureBrand

NTT docomo

NTT DoCoMo
Japan, 2008

TRACFNE

TracFone
USA

TalkTalk

TalkTalk
United Kingdom, 2006

debitel

debitel
Germany

VERTU

Vertu
United Kingdom

PANTECH

Pantech
South Korea

COMDIAL

Comdial
USA

E-Plus
Germany

544

Verizon
USA, 2000
Landor Associates, DeSola Group

OTE
Greece

HYT Radios
Australia

Nextel Communications
USA, 2011
Landor Associates

Nortel
USA, 1995
Siegel+Gale

Netopia
USA

Tenzing
USA

J-Sky
Japan

XO Communications
USA

ConTel
USA

Connex
Romania

Pacific Bell
USA, 1984

Comcast
USA, 1970s

Avaya
USA

NOKIA

Nokia
Finland, 1990s

Time Warner Cable
USA, 2009
The Brand Union

BT
United Kingdom, 1991
Wolff Olins

TECHNOLOGY

APPS
BROWSERS & SEARCH ENGINES
COMPUTER COMPANIES
E-COMMERCE
ELECTRONICS & HARDWARE
INTERNET PORTALS
GIG ECONOMY
MOBILE PHONES
SEMICONDUCTORS
SOCIAL MEDIA
SOCIAL NETWORKS
SOFTWARE
SYSTEM COMPANIES
STREAMING
VIDEO GAMES

Thunderbird
USA, 2011

Firefox 3.5
USA, 2009
The Iconfactory: Anthony Piraino,
Jon Hicks, Stephen Horlander

Google Earth
USA, 2010

Google Chrome
USA, 2011
Office, Google Creative Lab

iTunes
USA, 2006

iTunes
USA, 2010

Internet Explorer
USA

Lotus
USA, 1980s

Macromedia Flash 5
USA

Liquid Audio
USA

Cincom
USA

StumbleUpon
USA

c|net
USA, 1994

Wikimedia
USA, 2010
*Wikimedia Foundation:
Philip Metschan*

Futuremark Corporation
Finland

Skype
Luxembourg

Google

Google
USA, 1999
Ruth Kedar

eBay
USA, 2012
Lippincott

Gmail
USA, 2010
Google

eBay
USA, 1995
Bill Cleary

Pinterest

Pinterest
USA

Intershop
Germany, USA

my⌐____⌐

**Myspace
(launch logo)**
USA, 2010

Myspace
USA, 2010

**America Online
(AOL)**
USA, 2009
Wolff Olins

Magic Software
Israel

550

Thermo Electron Corporation
USA

ST
Switzerland

1c
Russia

Dend Media Services
Netherlands

Acer
Taiwan, 2011

TechCrunch (TC)
USA, 2011
Code & Theory

IBM
USA, 1972
Paul Rand

IBM
USA, 1956
Paul Rand

CA Computer Associates
USA, 2005
Sequel Studio

CA Computer Associates
USA, 2001
Landor Associates

Gerber Systems
USA

Maya Complete
USA

Dassault Systèmes
France

Maya
USA, 2017

National Semiconductor
USA

EIZO

Eizo
Japan

NCR

NCR
USA, 1996
Saul Bass

altavista

AltaVista
USA

NANYA

Nanya Technology
USA

YOKOGAWA

Yokogawa
Japan

altavista
SEARCH SOFTWARE

AltaVista
USA

AMERICA
Online

America Online
(AOL)
USA, 1991

AUTODESK

Autodesk
USA

Adobe

Adobe
USA, 1993

Autodesk
USA

Windows
USA, 2012
Pentagram: Paula Scher

NETSCAPE

Netscape
USA

Windows 3.0
USA, 1990

 **Agilent Technologies**

Agilent Technologies
USA

Ikusi
Spain

Topcon
USA

Cirrus Logic
USA

ST Ericsson
Switzerland

Frontier Silicon
United Kingdom

Parker
USA

Delta Dore
France

Analog Devices
USA

MICRON

Micron
USA

ACUSON

Acuson
USA

Towa
Japan

Dialogic

Dialogic Corporation
Canada, ca 2006

Xantech
USA

BARCO

Barco
Belgium

KEYENCE

Keyence
Japan

Mitutoyo

Mitutoyo
Japan

AIXTRON

Aixtron
Germany

BALLARD

Ballard Power Systems
USA

Deezer
France

Facebook
USA, 2005
Cuban Council: Joe Kral, Peter Markatos

tumblr.
USA

Autodesk
USA

Symantec
USA, 1990

NCR
USA

Tech Data
USA

Groupon
USA, 2008

ATI
USA

SAP
Germany, 2011

SAP
Germany, ca 2000
Frog Design

Beghelli
Italy

Krohne
Germany

Tokyo Electron
(TEL)
Japan

Virb
USA, 2007

Corel
USA, 2001

ELPIDA

Elpida
Japan

Adobe
USA, 1982
Marva Warnock

Advent Software
USA

ANDROID

Android
USA
Ascender Corporation

CHRISTIE

Christie
USA

Amazon
USA, 2000
Turner Duckworth: Anthony Biles

match.com

Match.com
USA

craigslist

Craigslist
USA

Daily**motion**

Dailymotion
France, 2005

Intel
USA, 2006
*FutureBrand: Sylvia Chu, Rebecca Cobb,
Ana Gonzalez, Isabella Ossott*

Intel Inside
USA, 2003

FlyerTalk
USA

RealPlayer
USA

Airbnb
USA

Napster
USA

reddit
USA

Delicious
USA, 2008

Blogger
USA

MSNBC
USA, 2007

Expedia.com
USA, 2010

Wanadoo
France, 1990s

WordPress
USA

Plaxo
USA

Play.com
United Kingdom

Picasa
USA

Windows
USA, 2001

Shimadzu
Japan

Bluetooth
USA, 1998

Symantec
USA, 2010

Steinberg
Germany

RealChat Software
USA

WorldCat.org
USA

Network Solutions
USA, 1990s

Network Solutions
USA, 2009
Pappas Group

Yahoo!
USA, 1996
Organic: Kevin Farnham, Geoff Katz
Yahoo!: David Shen

Vimeo
USA

Bing
USA, 2009
Razorfish

flickr
USA

Goo Software
United Kingdom
Jon Hicks

Sage
United Kingdom

FWA
United Kingdom, 2003
Dual

Cognos
USA

Netkey
USA

DeNA
Japan

Macromedia
USA, 1997

YouSendIt
USA

MSN
USA, 1999

MSN
USA, 2010
Microsoft

Overture Services
USA

Twitter
USA, 2010

Garmin
USA, 2006

Terra Networks
Spain
FutureBrand

LinkedIn
USA, 2003

YouTube
USA, 2006
Chad Hurley

Wikipedia
USA, 2010
Wikimedia Foundation: Philip Metschan

Quark
USA, 2005
SicolaMartin (Young & Rubicam)

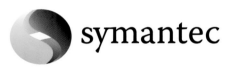

Symantec
USA, ca 2001
Interbrand

ACDSee
Canada

Ableton
Germany

Ableton Live
Germany

Adobe Postscript
USA

Adobe Acrobat
USA

Microchip Technology
USA

Digital River
USA

Oblicore
USA

Direct Print
Japan

Autodesk Maya
USA

Allume Systems
USA

McAfee Security
USA

566

Super Famicom
Japan, 1990

Expedia
USA

Qooq
France

Digg
USA

Adani
Belarus

Scala
USA

Google
(browser icon)
USA, 1999
Ruth Kedar

Spotify
Sweden/United Kingdom
Christian Wilsson, Rasmus Andersson

Android
USA, 2007
Irina Blok

Twitter
USA, 2007
Simon Oxley

PostgreSQL
USA

IBM Smarter Planet
USA, 2008
Studio Intraligi, Ogilvy

Big Websites
South Africa

Red Hat
USA, 1990s

**Facebook
(icon)**
USA
Future Farmers: Linda Leow

Instagram
USA, 2011

VERITAS

Veritas
USA

monster

Monster
USA

Intel
USA, 1968

Asus
Taiwan

intuit

Intuit
USA, 2008

smiths

Smiths
United Kingdom

CITRIX

Citrix
USA

Borland

Borland
USA

VERIO

Verio
USA

IKON

Ikon Office Solutions
USA

Ariba
USA, 1990s

AIM
(AOL instant messenger)
USA, 1990s

Hauri
South Korea

Green Hills
USA

Norton AntiVirus
USA

Mozilla Corporation
USA

OmniPage Pro
USA

ACT!
USA

EA Games
USA

Xbox 360
USA

EA
(Electronic Arts)
USA, 2006

EA Sports
USA, 1999

Xbox
USA

Alienware
USA

Square-Enix
Japan

DICE
(Digital Illusions Creative Entertainment)
Sweden, ca 2008

Valve Corporation
USA

Nintendo 64
Japan, 1996

Atari
USA, 1972
George Opperman

SEGA
Japan

Wii
Japan, 2006

Game Boy
Japan, 1989

Activision
USA

Coleco
USA

Nintendo
Japan, 2006

572

DJ Hero
USA, 2009

Guitar Hero
USA, 2005

Angry Birds
Finland, 2009
Rovio

Pokémon
Japan

Pac-Man
Japan, 1980

Vice City
(Grand Theft Auto)
United Kingdom

Street Fighter II
Japan, 1991

Konami
Japan, 1986

Dreamcast
Japan, 1998

SEGA Saturn
(Western logo)
Japan, 1995

Nichibutsu
Japan

Rockstar Games
USA

Bandai
Japan

Infogrames
France

Guerrilla Games
Netherlands, 2004

Left 4 Dead
USA, 2008

PlayStation
Japan, 1994
Manabu Sakamoto, Sony

Blizzard Entertainment
USA

PlayStation 2
Japan, 2000

PlayStation 3
Japan

Alien Skin Software
USA, 1993

Wolfenstein
USA, ca 2009

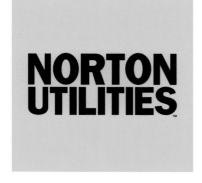

Super Nintendo Entertainment System
Japan, 1991

Vivendi Universal Games
France, 2002

NORTON
UTILITIES

Norton Utilities
USA

IFS Defence
Sweden

JBL

JBL
USA, 1968
Arnold Wolf

ELAC

ELAC
Germany

JVC

JVC
Japan

BenQ

BenQ
Taiwan

CASIO

Casio
Japan

EPSON

Epson
Japan

2Wire
USA

DIVX

DivX
USA

Bose
USA, 1960s

CHINON

Chinon
Japan

PHILCO

Philco
USA

GRUNDIG

Grundig
Germany

SHARP

Sharp
Japan

ZALMAN

Zalman
USA

TELEFUNKEN

Telefunken
Germany

Microsoft

Microsoft
USA, 1987
Scott Baker

Panasonic

Panasonic
Japan, 2007

LaserDisc

LaserDisc
Japan, 1990s

Packard Bell

Packard Bell
Netherlands, 2003

Discman

Discman
Japan, 2000

PowerPC

PowerPC
USA, 1992

Pioneer

Pioneer
Japan, 1998

Technics

Technics
USA

NETGEAR

Netgear
USA

MAGNAVOX

Magnavox
USA

Qume
USA

BRAUN
Braun
Germany, 1952
Wolfgang Schmittel

OMRON
Omron
Japan

TASCAM
Tascam
Japan

Kensington
Kensington
USA

Quantum
Quantum Corporation
USA

LEXMARK™
Lexmark
USA, 1994

KENWOOD
Kenwood
Japan

ZyLAB
ZyLAB
Netherlands

D-Link
D-Link
Taiwan

Clarion
Japan

Gateway
USA, 2002
Arnell Group

Cerner
USA, 1980s

Emerson Electronics
USA

Crown Audio
USA

ComTrade Group
Serbia

Olidata
Italy

Everex
Taiwan

Zune
USA

Funai
Japan

Monster Cable
USA

Blaupunkt
Germany

BlackBerry
Canada

Alpine
USA

Nakamichi
Japan

Clairtone
Canada, ca 1967
Burton Kramer

Vestax
Japan, 1970s

Tandem
USA

Rockford Fosgate
USA

ColorSync
USA

QuickTime
USA

Walkman
Japan
Hiroshige Fukuhara

Blu-ray Disc
USA

It's a Sony
Japan, 1982

AKG Acoustics
Austria, 1953

SPESCOM

Spescom
South Africa, 1970s

KEANE

Keane
USA

Packard Bell
Netherlands, 2009
Acer

dbx
USA, 1971

gradiente

Gradiente
Brazil

GRIFFIN

Griffin Technology
USA

584

Logitech

Logitech
Switzerland, 1988
Frog Design: Timothy Stebbing

Newton

Newton
USA, ca 1993

wacom

Wacom
Japan, 2007
Wolff Olins

Java

Java
USA

Cisco Systems
USA, 2006
Joe Finocchiaro, Jerry Kuyper

3Com
USA, 2000
Interbrand

Exabyte
USA

Commodore
Canada, 1985

NetApp
USA, 2008

Leading Edge
USA

Brondi
Italy

FWT Studios
United Kingdom

Tieto
Finland

586

NeXT Computer
USA, 1986
Paul Rand

Telefunken
Germany

Telex
USA

Commodore-Amiga
USA, 1980s

Lenoxx Sound
USA

Marantz
USA

BDNA
USA, 2008
Pentagram

Rowenta
Germany

Zenith Electronics
USA

Peavey
USA, ca 1965
Hartley Peavey

Energy
Canada

CONNER

Conner
USA

MTX Audio
USA

TrekStor

Trekstor
Germany

Maxtor
USA

matrox

Matrox
Canada

Digital 8
Japan, 1999

Data Cooler
Taiwan

Avid
USA, 2009
The Brand Union

SD Card
USA

ADP
USA

CORE Business Technologies
USA

Wega
Germany

CSC
(Computer Sciences Corporation)
USA, 1987
Robert Miles Runyon

Fujitsu
Japan, 1989

Sony
Japan, 1973
Yasuo Kuroki

Eiki
Japan

Akai
Japan

Aiwa
Japan, 2003

Vaio
Japan, 1996
Manabu Sakamoto

Bang & Olufsen
Denmark

**Japan Information
Processing Service**
Japan

SanDisk

SanDisk
USA, 2007
MetaDesign

ORACLE

Oracle
USA

FOSTEX

Fostex
Japan

maxell

Maxell
Japan

CREATIVE

Creative
Singapore

COMPAQ

Compaq
USA, 1999
Landor Associates

Acer
Taiwan, 2001

MSI
Taiwan, 2009

Dell
USA, 2009
Dell Global Creative

UMAX

UMAX
Taiwan

lenovo 联想

Lenovo Group
China

olivetti

Olivetti
Italy, 1970
Walter Ballmer

Avid

Avid
USA, 1980s

ICL

ICL
(International
Computers Ltd)
United Kingdom

WYSE

Wyse Technology
USA

measurex

Measurex
USA

mem⠶rex

Memorex
USA

GALAXY

Galaxy Technology
China

ONKYO

Onkyo
Japan

UNISYS

Unisys
USA

DENON

Denon
Japan

592

CSC
(Computer Sciences Corporation)
USA, 2008
Interbrand

RSA
USA

Atari
France, 2003

Vtech
China

Wang
USA, ca 1976

Digital
USA

Wacom
Japan

Olympus
Japan, 2001

U.S. Robotics
USA

GoVideo
USA

Binatone

Binatone
United Kingdom

Garrard

Garrard
United Kingdom

Ippon
Russia

SureFire
USA

bticino

Bticino
Italy

palmOne

PalmOne
USA, 2004

Haier

Haier
China

OAG
United Kingdom

Franklin
Computer

Franklin Computer
USA

CrossPad™
PORTABLE DIGITAL NOTEPAD

CrossPad
USA

Compact Disc
Netherlands, 1982

MiniDisc
Japan, 1992

VHS
(Video Home System)
Japan, 1976

ELSA
Germany/Taiwan

XLO Electric
Canada

MD Walkman
Japan

Linux Professional Institute
USA

Palm
USA, 2005
Turner Duckworth

HP
USA, 2008

LaCie
USA/France, 1995
Neil Poulton

Dell
USA, 1994

HP
USA, 2000

Corsair
USA

Viking Components
USA, 1988

FireWire
USA

Kenwood
Japan

SanDisk
USA

Seagate
USA, 2002
Landor Associates

Nvidia
USA, 2006

Iomega
USA

QLogic
USA

Gigabyte Technology
Taiwan

AMD
USA

Marmitek
Netherlands

 **Pitney Bowes**

Pitney Bowes
USA

D&B
Dun & Bradstreet

Dun & Bradstreet
USA, 1996
Landor Associates

 **adaptec**

Adaptec
USA

DataGeneral

Data General
USA

Verbatim

Verbatim
USA

DATACRAFT

Datacraft
South Africa

TDS **TELE DATA SYSTEM**

TDS Tele Data System
Czech Republic

NATIONAL INSTRUMENTS

National Instruments
USA

 *Sun* microsystems

Sun Microsystems
USA, 1990s

 **SIERRA WIRELESS**™

Sierra Wireless
Canada

Jeppesen
USA, 2008

Emerson Electronics
USA

Crestone International
USA

Network Appliance
USA

Nomaï
France

Labtec
USA

Data Return
USA

Stikk
Kosovo, 2009
projectGRAPHICS

Western Digital
USA, 2004

SyQuest
USA

Adata
Taiwan, 2010

MySQL
USA
Priority Advertising: Renne Angelvuo

Cherry
Germany

Ace Beepers Inc
USA

Skullcandy
USA

Linux mascot
(Tux the Penguin)
USA, 2006
Larry Ewing

Apple Computer Co.
USA, 1976
Ronald Wayne

Apple
USA, 1977
Regis McKenna Advertising:
Rob Janoff

Apple
USA, 1980s

Apple
USA

Mac
USA, 1997
Apple: Tom Hughes,
John Casado

Apple
USA, 2003

100 Illustrators

Illustration Now!
Portraits

Illustration Now!
Fashion

100 Manga Artists

Logo Design

Fritz Kahn.
Infographics Pioneer

Bodoni. Manual of
Typography

The Package Design
Book

D&AD.
The Copy Book

Menu Design
in America

1000 Tattoos

Bookworm's delight:
never bore, always excite!

TASCHEN
Bibliotheca Universalis

The Circus.
1870s–1950s

Mid-Century Ads

1000 Pin-Up Girls

20th Century Fashion

20th Century Travel

20th Century
Classic Cars

1000 Record Covers

Funk & Soul Covers

Jazz Covers

Extraordinary
Records

Steinweiss

Film Noir

Film Posters of the
Russian Avant-Garde

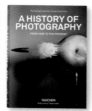
A History of
Photography

20th Century
Photography

100 Contemporary
Houses

100 Interiors Around
the World

Interiors Now!

The Grand Tour

Burton Holmes.
Travelogues

Living in Japan

Living in Morocco

Living in Bali

Living in Mexico

Living in Provence

Living in Tuscany

Tree Houses

Scandinavian Design

Industrial Design A-Z

domus 1950s

domus 1960s

Design of the
20th Century

1000 Chairs

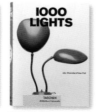
1000 Lights

Decorative Art 60s

Decorative Art 70s

2194

2195

2196

2198

2199

2200

2202

2203

2204

2206

2207

2208

Sure signs

Diverse logos from around the world

A good logo can glamorize just about anything. Now available in our popular *Bibliotheca Universalis* series, this sweeping compendium gathers diverse brand markers from around the world to explore the irrepressible power of graphic representation. Organized into chapters by theme, the catalog explores how text, image, and ideas distil into a logo across events, fashion, media, music, and retailers. Featuring work from both star names and lesser-known mavericks, this is an excellent reference for students and professionals in design and marketing, as well as for anyone interested in the visuals and philosophy behind brand identity.

"An excellent visual reference..."

—*Curve Magazine*, Sydney

Logo Design
Julius Wiedemann
664 pages
TRILINGUAL EDITION IN:
ENGLISH / DEUTSCH / FRANÇAIS

YOU CAN FIND TASCHEN STORES IN

Amsterdam
P.C. Hooftstraat 44

Berlin
Schlüterstr. 39

Beverly Hills
354 N. Beverly Drive

Brussels
Rue Lebeaustraat 18

Cologne
Neumarkt 3

Hamburg
Bleichenbrücke 1-7

Hollywood
Farmers Market,
6333 W. 3rd Street, CT-10

Hong Kong
Shop 01-G02 Tai Kwun,
10 Hollywood Road,
Central

London
12 Duke of York Square

London Claridge's
49 Brook Street

Miami
1111 Lincoln Rd.

"If browsing is considered an art form, the TASCHEN store is a masterpiece."
— *Dwell*

Milan
Via Meravigli 17

Paris
2 rue de Buci

**EACH AND EVERY TASCHEN BOOK
PLANTS A SEED!**
TASCHEN is a carbon neutral publisher.
Each year, we offset our annual carbon
emissions with carbon credits at the
Instituto Terra, a reforestation program
in Minas Gerais, Brazil, founded by
Lélia and Sebastião Salgado. To find out
more about this ecological partnership,
please check:
www.taschen.com/zerocarbon
**INSPIRATION: UNLIMITED.
CARBON FOOTPRINT: ZERO.**

To stay informed about TASCHEN
and our upcoming titles, please subscribe
to our free magazine at www.taschen.com/
magazine, follow us on Instagram and
Facebook, or e-mail your questions
to contact@taschen.com.

© 2021 TASCHEN GmbH
Hohenzollernring 53
D–50672 Köln
www.taschen.com

German Translation
Andrea Wiethoff for Delivering iBooks
& Design, Barcelona
French Translation
Valérie Lavoyer for Delivering iBooks
& Design, Barcelona

Printed in Bosnia-Herzegovina
ISBN 978–3–8365–7675–8